CHECKMATE

THE KING'S GAME
IN THE MIDDLE EAST

In the game of Chess, the Checkmate is a position
in which the King is threatened with capitulation,
and there is no way to remove the threat.
Checkmating wins
the game.

GENNARO BUONOCORE

ISBN: 978-1-7358535-0-5 (paperback) /
ISBN 978-1-7358535-1-2 (e-book)

First Edition

Library of Congress Control Number: 2020947150

Buonocore / Gennaro

Non-Fiction / Political Science / Military Studies / Adult Education

Book Summary: A comprehensive look into the current Middle Eastern political and strategic realities. Utilizes the game of chess to understand the relationship between the players of the region. Describes a part of the world where emotions, passions and cultural heritage have played the protagonists' roles. Considers historical implications, memories both physical and emotional, and the unfortunate consequences of cultural displacements, as it explores the effects on social identities, which may result in prolonged strife and conflict. This is a collection of personal observations and experiences placed in the context of historical events.

Published by Notable Publishing, PO Box 2047
Parker, Colorado 80134 / 303.840.5787

Printed in the United States of America

This book is dedicated to the five major pieces in my life:

*To my mother, the Bishop, Renata, who God entrusted
to bring me into a life during which I received
more than I could ever dream.*

*To my wife, the Queen, Cynni, who demonstrated that
the old Italian adage is correct—
"Masculinity bestows masculinity, but it takes an
exceptional woman to make an exceptional man."*

*To my two sisters, the Rooks, Stefania and Marirosa,
who have been always ready to "castle" in my defense.*

*To the United States of America, my adoptive warrior King,
because, as the Turks say—
"It is the battle that makes the warrior."*

Table of Contents

"What you see is transitory. What
you hope for is eternal."
— Fr. Peter Kirwin OFM

Foreword

"[The United States] is a gigantic boiler.
Once the fire is lighted under it, there is no limit
to the power it can generate."
— Edward Gray

EXPLAINING THE COMPLEX intricacies of this book or the daedal mind of its author could justifiably consume many pages. But, for the reader's benefit and bearing in mind the importance of brevity in any foreword, I am delighted to offer both a modicum of insight into the author's persona and some pithy thoughts on his most recent work. *Checkmate,* in a sublimely captivating way, explains the geopolitical state of play that has shaped U.S. national security planning for the last two decades.

Over the last 22 years in uniform, I have learned a great deal—most notably, the ability to understand and operate effectively in a joint-warfare environment and an appreciation for the aspects of tactical, operational, and strategic levels of war. After many joint assignments, I can attest to the benefits of a broad-minded understanding of how U.S. armed forces interrelate.

I am grateful for assignments in each level of warfare: tactically, as a wartime pilot, as an operational planner on multiple four-star staffs, and in strategic advisory positions at the National Security Council, the State Department, and the Department of Defense—all focused on the Middle East Area of Operations. I have been honored to serve my

country in intellectually stimulating and deeply fulfilling roles. Each
has afforded me chances to meet, challenge, and learn from dedicated
and thoughtful people at the highest levels of our government. I have
also benefited from relationships with especially skillful colleagues
in the trenches. Foremost among this group is Gennaro Buonocore.

I first met Gennaro at a command sponsored *Iftar* dinner, a religious observance of *Ramadan,* where Muslims gather to break their
fast. I had been assigned to U.S. Central Command headquarters in
Tampa, Florida, as the Coalition Operations Branch Chief.

Gennaro had been assigned as my deputy, and I knew that he
would be working the event. Dressed in his *thobe, ghutra,* and *egal,*
he casually navigated the room and found ways to repeatedly insert
himself into conversations, asking penetrating questions to our commander, General Joseph Votel, and various international officers six
pay grades his senior. Gennaro's timing was flawless and his execution
perfectly natural. I knew he had been trained as a Foreign Area Officer
(FAO), but there was something very distinctive about this military
diplomat. I was observing personality nuances I had not seen in the
defense attachés, security-cooperation officers, and political-military
planners I knew. In Gennaro, I saw a man determinedly searching for
answers to his *own* strategic questions—not necessarily those of the
Department. In addition, I saw a man genuinely enjoying the search.

I worked closely with Gennaro for more than two years.
Charismatic and savvy by nature, he used his business background
to develop strategies for soliciting offerings from our coalition partners to resource our combined operations in Iraq and Syria. Middle
East partners presented challenges in this area, but Gennaro was
undeterred. He exhibited complete command of the complex issues
associated with resourcing a combined operation while maintaining a
broad, strategic understanding of the partnered operations required to
execute the campaign plan. He understood the vital linkages among
military objectives and political obstacles better than most flag officers.
I would often find him in the coalition spaces, sipping lemon-mint

with a Qatari general, *raki* with a Turkish non-commissioned officer, or coffee with a Saudi Arabian defense official. Every touchpoint provided him with nuanced information he would use to refine his sales approach for each partner nation.

Gennaro performed as a seasoned soldier-statesman with a deft, fingertip feel for the pulse of every senior officer from every Middle East nation. Whether it was his international upbringing, regional experience, or just plain charisma, Gennaro was a trusted friend to every coalition partner in Tampa—particularly those from the Levant and the Arabian Peninsula.

Checkmate uses the game of chess to weave together the multifaceted relationships of various nation states. Game figurines, each with its own strengths and limitations, represent the major players in the Middle East today.

The parallels among chess and geopolitics abound. China and Russia are knights—very powerful pieces in the midst of a busy chess board, but very weak on an open board. The metaphor holds true as these nations play opportunist and spoiler in the midst of chaos but are ineffective and unwilling to lead when exposed.

The rooks, pieces generally inactive during the opening—but crucial players in every endgame—represent Iran and Egypt. These two nations will have a say in the ultimate fate of the Middle East. Turkey and Israel are depicted by bishops, chess pieces with immense power on an open board. In the game of chess, two bishops working together can dominate a match. Might that mutually beneficial synergy someday translate to these regional powers? The likelihood of these two nations working in lockstep is low, but they do have strong common interests and a compelling history. Turkey was, after all, the first Muslim majority country to recognize the state of Israel.

Finally, America is appropriately typecast as Queen—the only chess piece with the ability to perpetually check an opponent's king. A strong case is made for a continued U.S. force presence in the region. America needs to stay in the game.

Gennaro's upbringing, military service, love for history, and ability to understand people make him uniquely qualified to write this book. It marks his latest national security accomplishment in his quest to increase the distance between shouting and shooting in the Middle East. I urge every U.S. service-member, diplomat, and national-security professional to grab *Checkmate*, settle in, and enjoy.

Tony Schwarz, Captain, United States Navy
Senior Military Advisor
Middle East Policy
Office of the Secretary of Defense

Captain Anthony (Tony) Schwarz, a naval aviator with combat tours under his belt, is a graduate of the U.S. Naval Academy. He has graduate degrees in Organizational Management from George Washington University and in National Security and Strategic Studies from the Naval War College. He has attended the Leadership Development program at Harvard's Kennedy School. Schwarz has served on multiple staffs—at the White House as Executive Assistant to Dr. Meghan O'Sullivan, Deputy National Security Advisor for Iraq and Afghanistan; as a Military Advisor to the Office of Iraqi Affairs at the State Department, where he represented Secretaries Powell and Rice in congressional meetings, drafted policy documents, and assisted in the development of Iraqi Security Force training; as the Branch Chief for international coalition force generation at the United States Central Command during Operation Inherent Resolve. He currently serves in the Middle East Policy Directorate of the Office of Secretary of Defense.

Preface

"That which causes men to become a
people is not only the recollection of great
things they have done together, but the
longing and the will to do new things..."
What Is a Nation? by French historian Ernest Renan
(1823–1892)

I FINISHED THIS BOOK in the period between June 2019 and February
2020 as I started connecting all the pertinent facts upon my return
to civilian life following a long period of military duty in the service
of the United States Central Command.

I asked someone of whom I am very fond to edit the manuscript.
I did it for a number of reasons—he is an excellent writer, and his
command of the English language is the result of years of academic
knowledge and teaching. His American writing style is direct and
concise, therefore completely different from my Mediterranean narration style. He also believes that *"one should believe nothing of what
one is told and half of what one sees."*

Some books are meant to be read; others are meant to be *studied*.
I believe that this book is meant to be studied. Although its content may
be very familiar to those who are already somewhat acquainted with
the dynamics of the area, I have purposefully stayed out of extensive
details to cater to those who haven't benefitted from exposure to the
Middle East. Every statement that I make deserves further research

and challenge, because this is not an easy subject. It is highly subjective and too important for humanity, as so much blood has been spilled in the Middle East over the past 4000 years.

I have been attracted to the Middle East from an early age. My middle-school-graduation project was on Saudi Arabia. That was 40 years ago. Since then, I have studied many books on the subject and read everything I could get my hands on. Former U.S. Secretary Of Defense Jim Mattis once said: *"If you haven't read hundreds of books, you are functionally illiterate, and you will be incompetent, because your personal experiences alone aren't broad enough to sustain you."*

In this light, I recently studied a book—*"Zealot"* by Reza Aslan. It is a political investigation into the historical *Yeshua bar Joseph an Nahzri* and the difference with the theological and spiritual Jesus Christ of the canonic Gospels. Had I not *studied* (rather than read) the book, I would have had to choose between the faith I profess and the historical science behind Aslan's investigation. Because I am studying it, I can perceive how Aslan lovingly honored Yeshua (Jesus), by revealing a very different personage from the peace-loving Messiah of modern Christianity. There are different ways of reaching reality, of achieving truth. Only the incurable ignorant claims omniscience.

Most of the background material for this book had been collected over the prior five years, but I could never tie all that I had memorialized into a cohesive message. Two very distinct yet very connected events gave me the incentive to finally start writing: a meeting with an Egyptian scholar in Cairo, who explained to me what he believed was the meaning of "home" and a conversation on the meaning of "roots" with my elderly mother.

With time, my life memories, even those very distant in age, are becoming clearer, and they are serving me by providing answers to questions that I have left unanswered for the past fifteen years—questions about the meaning of home, my roots, what constitutes success, and about war and justice.

Also, very impactful but of a completely different nature were the experiences during my participation in the D-ISIS (Defeat of the Islamic State of Iraq and Syria) campaign, from March 2015 to May 2019. What I witnessed during those four years triggered the desire to seek alternative answers to the bloodshed that I had already witnessed in Iraq and in Afghanistan, during what the Arabs call the *Third Gulf War* and we called *Operation Iraqi Freedom,* and during Afghanistan's *Enduring Freedom.*

The material underpinning for this book comes from those war experiences, from traveling and working around the globe, from teaching Comparative National Security Analysis at Excelsior College, and from my craft as a reserve Foreign Area Officer in the United States Navy.

My writing style reflects my cultural background; it is, according to my editor and to book critics, *"verbose, flowery, arabesque, and prone to hyperboles"*—a very common style in the Mediterranean and in the Arab world. This communication style suits patient people.

The styles of other writers whom I quote in the book are also very different, according to their cultural backgrounds. For example, although they have lived all over the world, *Sameer Baitamouni,* a Syrian, and *Francesco Guerrera,* an Italian, have very similar Mediterranean writing styles, just as hyper-descriptive as mine. Others, especially the Anglo-Saxons and the Northern Europeans, are more concise and straight to the point. One must bear in mind that writing styles are an indicator of how people think and communicate. We should always read plenty of literature originating from the regions which we are analyzing, as it reveals mindsets, customs, and traditions.

There is nothing "concise and straight to the point" when it comes to the Middle East. There are no available short-cuts; understanding that area of the world requires in-depth study and great patience.

I have always liked playing chess. I am a very average player, but understanding how crafty and complicated the game can get, makes me appreciate good players and masters even more. The game of chess, just like the Arabic and Mediterranean communication style, suits patient people.

Chess is a strategic board game possibly derived from the Indian *chaturanga* in 600 AD. It is believed to have been imported into Europe in the 9th century. The "importers" were *Andalus Umayyad* Arabs of southern Spain. Those who have played chess agree that it requires strategy, foresight, and a tactical understanding of the "line" and of the playing field. This grasp cannot be complete without having mastered the understanding of the characteristics, powers, and inter-operability of each chess piece in the line.

As I always found the game very fascinating, I was one of those kids glued to the black-and-white television screen, enthralled by the epic 1978 battle between Viktor Korchnoi and Anatoli Karpov. These chess masters were, for me, like mythological figures: warriors whose superpowers were superior intellect, cunning, and coolness under extreme pressure—true *speznats* of the chessboard like Kasparov, Spassky, Kavalek, Harandi, and the unforgettable Bobby Fischer. Their matches had the taste of Cold War and international intrigue. The Fischer vs Spassky 1972 *"Match of the Century"* ended the 24-year Soviet international domination of the game. I was too young then, but I was told by my father that it was like seeing the U.S. Central Intelligence Agency battling the Soviets' *Komitet Gosudarstvennoy Bezopasnosti,* in front of millions of spectators.

During that time, which now seems magical to me, we were watching Italian newscasts that kept referring to the *Scacchiere Mediorientale*—The Middle Eastern Chessboard. The *telegiornale*—the television news—brought legendary figures into our living rooms: Sadat, Moshe Dayan, Abu Nidal, Kissinger, Rabin, Yasser Arafat, King Hussein of Jordan, Reza Pahlavi, Jimmy Carter. It was, for us spectators, an incredible chess game, intriguing to say the least.

For millennia, the Middle East has been a geopolitical and strategic chessboard where states, like chess pieces exercise different levels of influence and power, largely dependent upon their material capability and proficiency in using elements of power.

After the breakup of the Ottoman Empire and a 30-year interlude dominated by the Great Britain/France *entente*, the preponderance of power continues to lie in the hands of a single piece, the *Queen*—the United States of America. The USA dominates in most aspects of national power, and its preferences keep prevailing in the present and, at least, for the near future.

The USA's historically unprecedented power structure allows it to act, at times, unilaterally. This attitude, as it was in the case of the Roman and Ottoman empires, is seen with ambivalence by the other pieces on the chessboard. If, on one hand, it prompts respect and deference, on the other, it fosters mistrust and outright resentment when unilateral actions are believed to be motivated by an entitled impunity, which breaks established local socio-geographical rules, without fear of retribution.

This book will not address whether America should or should not play the Queen's role in the Middle East. It seems that, in today's age, public opinion is split right down the middle on this matter. I believe that the price of greatness is global engagement, and I am one of the believers in American exceptionalism—a primacy that does not preclude the utmost respect for all other world cultures. I see my adoptive country's ideal role as the protector rather than the bully.

When describing foreign policy, it is difficult to steer clear of political commentary. I have attempted to stay out of the traditional partisan diatribe about the merits or demerits of American administrations. I do believe that the Middle East nut is very difficult to crack for anyone. There are no absolute truths in the Middle East and no ideal policies—only better policies and bad policies. Although some of my opinions might seem partisan, I have tried to frame my statements within the context of historical analysis.

Historically, the Middle Eastern major regional pieces have been dissatisfied with their status in the system, and they display eagerness to acquire similar advantages, which leads to competition. Currently, the only real threat for the chessboard's major power should be another major power. However, China and Russia—the knights—have no real ability to fully replace the Queen.

In the Middle East, it is widely believed that the only real *Achille's heel* for the USA are the USA's policies. At the regional level, Middle Eastern countries face multiple threats. They must deal not only with security threats stemming from global actors and regional rivals but also with internal dynamics, triggered by the spillover effects of regional conflicts, ethno-sectarian rifts, or social resentments. Also, for these countries, economic development remains, as much as security, a top priority.

Historically, in order to mitigate these risks, regional players, like states and tribes, pursue diverse strategies in accordance with their needs and concerns. Based on the level of national power, these pieces are either the audience or the active participants in the major power competition in the Middle East. They are in constant struggle between the needs for autonomy versus security and the fear of abandonment versus entrapment. The degree of national power (economic, military, informational, and diplomatic) and their ability to cope with perceived threats determine their position on the spectrum.

This book is about explaining the current Middle Eastern political and strategic reality as if we were looking at a gigantic chessboard. However, it is important to understand that strategy, in the Middle East, is not everything. This is an area where emotions, passions, and cultural heritage have informed the protagonists' roles.

It is also about historical implications, memories both physical and emotional, and the unfortunate consequences of cultural displacements. Their effect on social identities might result in prolonged strife and conflict. I did not attempt to write a sociology treatise or a policy paper. It is a collection of personal observations and experiences placed in the context of historical events. It focuses on the Middle East, but the concept could be applied to any area of the world.

With this book, I would like to suggest that conflict in the greater Middle East cannot be mitigated until Western expectations are modified to include an understanding of the effects that cultural heritage has on regional dynamics. If we wish to understand why we have lost so many lives (and caused the death of many more) with little to no progress toward lasting peace in the Middle East, we need to expand our understanding of cultural heritage to embrace a wider context that today's Western—and especially the American—culture does not easily provide. It is not necessarily the West's fault; it is just a natural consequence of beneficial economic development and secularization.

Conflict in the Middle East, especially in the Israeli-Palestinian conflict, cannot be effectively mitigated until America (the area's main player since the end of World War II and Israel's greatest sponsor) creates policies which address the grave damage to the Arabs' cultural heritage and its severe consequences on the stability and peace of that area.

The book will attempt to speak from a layman's perspective of "home" and "roots"; the lasting impact that losing these important life pillars could have on individual and collective identity; and the desperate attempt to find them again. I am myself a cultural-heritage orphan, but I have been lucky and resilient enough to find purpose. In the first chapter, I write at length about my own heritage and my sense of loss, which hardly compares to a Palestinian or an Iraqi who have lost their homes and families.

Despite this great difference, I have applied my own perception of the value of home—memories, relationships, and opportunities—and put myself in the shoes of a Syrian, an Iraqi, a Palestinian, or an Israeli, attempting to understand what it feels like to lose everything. Would I fight? Almost certainly, yes.

Like the other two books I have previously authored, this one contains testimonies from people who are weighing in on the matter through the filter of their own experiences. At times, these people's opinions might differ from mine, but that is the nature of things—absolute truth is somewhat of an abstract concept.

From 2015 to 2020, I designed and taught a course entitled "BNS303—The Comparative National Security Analysis" at Excelsior College, in the USA. While a limited amount of material included in this book is attributable to this course, none of the opinions expressed in the book are necessarily the opinions of Excelsior College or its trustees, officers, employees, or agents.

When I teach the Comparative National Security Analysis craft to my budding analysts, I always ask them to use *Maslow's Hierarchy of Needs* whenever they look at societies, individuals, and cultures. It helps them not only in the class environment and in their (mostly military) professions but in their lives in general.

I encourage the reader of this book to do the same, as I have not found a better tool than Maslow's pyramid to comprehend human beings at their different stages of life. Nations are made of people, and national policies are just the result of the balance between public and national interests.

The other concept I focus on is the DIME analysis of national power: how a nation uses the combination of Diplomatic, Informational, Military, and Economic policies as its tools of national power. All the actors in the Middle East use a combination of these tools.

From 2004, I have operated across the Middle East, first as a Civil Affairs officer in the Military Corps of the Italian Red Cross, an auxiliary unit in the Italian armed forces, and then as a United States naval officer. While a lot of what I write is heavily influenced by my experiences in these three capacities, none of the opinions expressed in this book are necessarily the opinions and policies of the United States Department of Defense or the government of the United States.

I would like to thank all the foreign military officers with whom I have worked and who have become my friends. I have treasured their insight, whether it was divulged in unclassified reports open to the public, and from which I generously borrowed, or from private conversations which transcended "party lines." For your willingness to confide in me so that I could truly see your point of view, I will forever be grateful. The names of these exceptional officers I cannot disclose, for privacy reasons, but you know who you are. You make your countries and your national armed forces proud of having such great talent amongst their ranks.

One of the most quotable quotes of the 20th century was attributed to a Chinese leader. When, during a February 1972 meeting between U.S. President Richard Nixon and the Chinese premier Zhou Enlai, a French reporter asked about the consequences of the French Revolution, Zhou Enlai is reputed to have said: *"It is too early to say."*

Coming as it did from China's foremost diplomat, it sounded profound. It became an example of the far-sighted nature of Chinese leaders, who thought in centuries, as opposed to the short-termism of Western politicians. The question was asked in 1972, and the French Revolution had occurred almost two hundred years before.

The concept it conveys applies perfectly to the Middle East, where sudden moves might have short immediate consequences but whose real effects might surface only centuries later.

However, there is even more pertinence to the Middle East, as it appears that the Chinese leader was not referring to the 1789 French Revolution but to the much more recent French students' revolts in 1968. Richard Nixon's translator was present at the meeting and came out to set the record straight. In the Middle East, whether it is accurate or not, the actual version of the occurrence changes significance according to the beholder.

Some misquotes are just too good to be corrected. Misquotes are part of history, and history is full of misunderstandings. It is true that, if we do not comprehend the past, we are likely to make unnecessary mistakes, however, mistakes are very much part of history, and humans do not all see the same story in the same way.

It is my firm belief that, when it comes to the Middle East, we are merely at the beginning of a one-hundred-year (at a minimum) war against militant Islamist Jihadism, a cultural and ideological movement that has every sociological reason to exist and that is here to stay for the foreseeable future. We need to challenge our understanding of "end-state." I believe that we are in no position, so early in the game, to correctly define what an appropriate end-state looks like.

When we are called to analyze realities, we should not fail to remember that we tend to see the world through the eyes of our social identity. Furthermore, I am convinced that we cannot understand ourselves if we do not understand others and vice-versa.

Getting to know others requires avoiding the twin dangers of overestimating either how much we have in common or how much divides us. Our shared humanity and the perennial issues which affect life mean that we can always learn from and identify with the thoughts and practices of others, no matter how alien they might first appear. At the same time, differences in ways of thinking can be both deep and subtle.

If we assume too readily that we can see things from others' points of view, we might easily end up seeing them from merely a variation of our own. Additionally, most of us suffer from restless minds that need to name everything, attempting to make something knowable, perhaps in the futile attempt to have power over it. The foremost question we should always ask when we look at something is: "Do I really know what I am looking at even when I am looking at it?"

It is also very important to carefully discern which sources of information we use. Impartial reporting no longer exists; I might argue that it never existed. I do not believe that there is a particularly nefarious intent behind this reality—human beings have a tendency to make their minds up, and, once they have done so, they have a natural reluctance to allow in information which is not in line with their beliefs. We are born believers, in terms of cognitive efforts, neuroscience tells us, and it is easier for us to believe than to remain skeptical.

That is why I am advising you to check the validity of facts that I am presenting in this book by extensively consulting other sources and by traveling to the Middle East and exploring it at length.

A word of final caution when reading literature about the Middle East. The Western spelling of Arab words is not consistent at all. Lawrence of Arabia used to mention that, because there is little resemblance between how *Franks* and Arabs phonetically pronounce the same words, expecting a uniform way to see these words typed is the same as expecting the desert sands to never shift.

Where the Light Is Liquid

"Lo there do I see my father; Lo there do
I see my mother and my sisters and my
brothers; Lo there do I see the line of
my people, back to the beginning.

Lo, they do call to me, they bid me take my
place among them, in the halls of Valhalla,
where the brave may live forever."

The 13th Warrior—1999

IT IS A VERY FUNDAMENTAL, easy-to-grasp concept—in today's age and throughout history—that identity is a human being's most prized possession. I am breaking with Maslow's theory just once by stating that the need for identity might be as physiological as the needs to eat, sleep, and be safe.

The fear or the perceived reality of losing identity can have very serious psychological consequences. Most of the world's conflicts are fueled by a people's perceived loss of identity and by a desperate attempt to fill the void.

Identity and the concept of a man's "home" are closely associated.

Home and identity rest on three pillars—memories, relationships, and opportunities. These pillars are not independent of each other. They are correlated and equally important. They are interchangeable only for a period. Take those three pillars away from a human being, and the house in which the individual is currently staying might come

1

down. Furthermore, if an individual who has lost everything has the courage, the desperation, and the strength of the biblical *Samson*, the house might come down with all the *Philistines* in it.

What are these identity and home concepts, and what do they mean to a human being?

Positive identity is the combination of treasured memories, cherished relationships, and honest opportunities—the home which nests and sustains an individual when all else falls apart, when life fades, when death is near.

There is a subtle yet substantial difference between a human being's identity and his/her character. Human character has been described as the consequence of DNA, environment, and learned behaviors. Character is a good indicator of someone's potential behavior—it is a human being's "script," his life toolbox.

Identity/home is a human being's essence, his/her refuge, his/her nest.

I left the Italian *Sud* (South), my home, in August 1987. I specify *Southern Italy* because, especially in the context of this book, the regionalization of memories is very relevant. Thirty-five years later, I would like to believe that I am clear on where I came from and where my home is.

I have been often called "Italian" or "Italian American," but I am not sure whether my heritage was ever truly Italian, as I do not know what "being Italian" really means. I rarely contradict those who speak about my *Italian-ness,* because it would take too long to explain that, because I am from Portici, a satellite city of greater Naples, nestled right underneath the great volcano that destroyed *Herculaneum* and *Pompeii*, I am a Son of the *Vesuvius*, a Neapolitan. I was born a Neapolitan, in a family that has been exclusively Neapolitan since the time we could trace our ancestry back to the end of 1400.

In a 1990 interview with American broadcaster Barbara Walters, Sofia Scicolone, whom most Americans know as Sofia Loren, when asked about her Italian descent, stated: *"I am not Italian. I am*

Neapolitan. It's another thing." I completely understood what she meant by *"It's another thing."* We Neapolitans are just *different*—very different. I call it "identification by negation." Neapolitans think differently, they speak a different language, they relate to each other differently, and they have completely different social and ethical codes than their Italian cousins. I will elaborate further on this "identification by negation" a bit later.

Neapolitans are a breed apart—the result of millennia of intertwining between Greeks, Romans, Normans, Saracens, and Spaniards—a new addition to a nation, Italy, which is barely is 159 years old, a mere milli-second in the history of the Mediterranean.

I grew up during a time when the actions of the *Brigate Rosse* and the *Nuclei Armati Rivoluzionari* in Italy, the *The Baader Meinhoff* and the *Rote Armee Fraktion* in Germany and *Action Directe* in France, the *Irish Republican Army* (IRA), and the *Euskadi Ta Askatasuna* (ETA) in Spain were leaving countless bodies in the streets of Rome, Paris, London, Munich, and Madrid.

The consequences of World War II had left Europe in a political turbulence which had fueled several lingering internal conflicts. Some thought that the spoils of war and the reconstruction effort had been very unequally allocated, and all for political reasons.

Some elements of society, political factions, or entire populations were left out of the rebuilding process for partisan reasons. Regional cultures, minorities, and political forces feared for their survival and their very own identity existence. They felt unjustly penalized and were seeking vindication by using force.

Were they terrorists or freedom fighters?

It depended on whom you asked. In Italy, which has the second-oldest aging population in the world behind Japan, one might ask this very question to any two Italian *baby boomers* and be certain to obtain two very different opinions.

From July 1970 to February 1971, in the south of Italy, the town of *Reggio Calabria* revolted because of a government decision to make

Catanzaro, a much smaller town, the regional capital of *Calabria*. The nomination of a regional capital was the result of a decentralization program by the Italian government to change the balance of power across the country in order to cement the control of a newly installed central government.

The Italian South, with its traditional baronial power structure, had voted in favor of the monarchy during the postwar referendum. The hotly contested results of that referendum had created the modern Italian republic. To this new political reality, the destabilizing domestic presence of communist, monarchist, and neo-fascist forces was a survival threat.

It was at this very important moment that the United States of America played a great, long-term positive role in the stabilization of postwar Italy and its new democracy. It was my first experience with the very positive role that America can play in the world. To my isolationist compatriots, I say that I owe my freedom to America. Global engagement is the price of a nation's greatness.

This is important to me because, 74 years later, America is still very present in Italy. This is proof of the successful application of engagement policies, and we should pause and reflect on the long-term merits of seeking quicker exits from other areas of the world that America has helped to democratize.

The obvious positive result of America's continuous engagement and policing in Europe was the elimination of political terrorism. There were also some downsides, such as the propping up of a dysfunctional democracy whose central-government legitimacy is still unproven in the *Meridione* (the Italian South), 74 years later. The glaring proof is the continued existence and the power of organizations like the Sicilian *Mafia*, the Calabrese *'Ndrangheta*, the Neapolitan *Camorra*, and the Pugliese *Sacra Corona Unita*. However, I will always prefer a dysfunctional democracy to a national-socialist dictatorship.

Having grown up in Italy, I have witnessed firsthand the unintended results of domestic policies that were created ignoring regional identities for the sake of "unity" and that were not focused at preserving and empowering the cultural heritage of human beings. Many southern Italians who were not feeling part of this new, mandated home, decided to emigrate. To be fair, the new Italian republican administration was full of southerners, however, most of them had given in to personal greed and *Mafia*'s pressures and had positioned their constituencies' needs as secondary to myopic short-term benefits.

I experienced a similar dynamic in post-Saddam Iraq.

Those who decided not to emigrate and remain in their heartland, despite difficult economic circumstances, managed to retain a sense of normalcy. Those who departed initially attempted to take "home"—their customs and their roots—with them. It is a typical coping mechanism—an attempt at alleviating the pain of separation.

I do not feel that, when people emigrate to a new land, they purposely wish to marginalize themselves by creating pockets of diversity. Everyone is merely drawn to what is familiar and welcoming.

I have met Italian-American families who are still living the traditions of a Sicily that their families left at the beginning of 1900. To me, they have the feel of a black-and-white picture in a multicolored world of globalized realities. Italian is not in their language repertoire—they speak either English or Sicilian, the dialect of their forefathers.

There is seldom an attempt at being identified as Italians, perhaps with the sole exception of when the Italian football national team is playing in the World Cup. That is because that team is traditionally one of the strongest in the world and, therefore, an affiliation to be proudly claimed.

Even when migrating within Italy, across this imaginary border just north of Rome, we were provided with an even starker reminder that Neapolitans are *another thing*. When leaving our homeland in search of better opportunities, whether we wished to integrate into other Italian cultures or not, we were never made to feel other than different. To Italian northerners, we were always *terroni* (peasants), no matter which social class we actually belonged to. We were made to feel different at every turn. Some of us really resented it—others, like me, made it a badge of pride.

In 1973, in Naples, we had a cholera outbreak. The United States Navy promptly sent medical teams to provide vaccines and other help in fighting the pandemic. My parents sent my sister and me, with my *nonna* (grandmother), to stay with extended family in the *Marche* region. When our accents gave up our provenience, we would not be allowed into shops, restaurants, or *caffe'*. People would barely greet us at a distance—or not at all— and even friends of our family would not shake *nonna's* hand. I was nine years old, but I will never forget that it was the United States Navy that came to my people's rescue and that we were treated as lepers by those who were meant to be our co-nationals.

Even if I wanted to forget, I am not allowed to. During the following 40 years, whenever the Napoli football team plays in a northern stadium, the chants of *colerosi, earthquake refugees, dirty, unwashed, beings who should be washed by the Vesuvius lava* are an omnipresent reality.

Forty-seven years later, the Italian North became the epicenter of the COVID-19 virus pandemic. The South was not as affected. After an initial response of *"Northerners, please stay in the North,"* the Southern identity came out: *"We don't do that. We are not Northerners."*

The *"We are another thing"* is a very common identification tool. It is not only party to the Neapolitan identity; I called it *the identification through negation*. We are *Neapolitans* because we are not *Milanese*. We are like this, as we are not like them. The *identification through negation* is something that I have encountered all over the world. It is generally accompanied by justifications of painful memories, stories which are dutifully passed from generation to generation. Stories about being wronged are not allowed to be forgotten: *"We Palestinians are not like the Jews. Look at what the Jews do to good people." "The Turks can't ever be trusted; they are a*

*bunch of murderers. Look at what they have done to us Armenians."
"The world is out to get us. Don't ever forget what was done to us during the holocaust. It is clear that we are not like them."*

For better economic opportunities, my father moved my family from Naples to Rome, when I was 10 years old. A mere 110 miles separate two different worlds. Albeit substantially different from ours, the somewhat elitist Roman attitude is one of initial distrust followed by acceptance and assimilation. If you identify yourself as a citizen of the *Roma Caput Mundi*—the *Roma Capitale*—then you are Roman, too. The same principle has applied to Roman citizens through the millennia of *Latin Rights*. I spent ten great years in the Eternal City, and that place is now my home as much as Napoli.

But it was still not so when I turned 20. After serving my obligation to the melting pot of the Italian Armed Forces, I left to look for opportunities in the United Kingdom.

My intention was to return home to work in the family business, after completing my education in Great Britain. I never did. I visited my original family often, but I never fully returned. Home became where I found opportunities for employment and where I created my own family—the United Kingdom first and then America.

Making your original family second to your acquired family is a cultural *faux pas* in the Italian South; in the eyes of the church, it is a cardinal sin. In the eyes of my original family, the Anglo-Saxon environment that had offered me the opportunity to excel materially had provided me also with the justification to sin. A typical show of love from my people is the attitude that, if you do something stupid, you always get the benefit of the doubt, and it must be somebody's else fault. My original family admired my success and praised my courage to seek it elsewhere, but I was still a prodigal son.

Very similarly, the Bedouin Arabs believe that a good and honorable life is possible only within the confines of one's own community and that *muzabin* like me, despite their material success, are constantly tasting *balash*—social death.

The importance of understanding of how human beings stack their priorities when it comes to allegiance is very vital. This personal life experience became very important when I had to deal with tribalism in the Sunni area of Al Anbar, in Iraq. I will expand on this later.

After I had spent almost double the time away from my original home creating a new one, I started missing my past more and more. The older I got, the more vivid my memories appeared, soothing me in difficult moments, sustaining me through the passing of time, and helping me accept the inevitability of old age. Those memories and the relationships that come with them remind me of who I am.

When I seek answers to important questions, I remember that, although I am American, I am also the result of 3,000 years of relations between Mediterranean races. I am part Greek, and, therefore, I am at ease in noisy and theatrical environments; I easily philosophize and find humor in everything. I am part Arab, so I adore the smells and the noise of crowded markets, the relentless bargaining, zipping on a scooter amongst the crazy road traffic, and the sun setting over the sea, whether it is made of water or sand dunes. I am part Spanish, as my faith is steeped in ancient, paganism-infused Catholic worship, where the cult of the dead is a constant reminder of the gift of being alive.

My first language is not English, not even Italian. It is Neapolitan, a language that has been classified as endangered by UNESCO. It is a mix of Italian, Spanish, Arabic, and French words which I punctually revert to when I communicate with my friends and family, and when my emotions run high.

Most of the statements I have made above carry a memory: the recalling of a relationship, a place, a smell. Leave those behind, and you risk carrying a hole within you, wherever you go.

This "hole" I speak of appeared to me later in life, between my late 20s and early 30s, when *my belly was very full* and while living the frenetic life of a bond salesman in the City of London. During that early period of my adulthood, I did not have the benefit of life experience and could not fully comprehend the malaise that I was experiencing—the sense of emptiness that I kept carrying around despite earning a lot of money and filling my life with all sorts of material comforts.

I was not alone in this. There were many more successful expatriates who were experiencing the same void.

I came across a *Financial Times* article by *Francesco Guerrera*, who was, at that time, the British newspaper's finance editor in the U.S. It was titled *"Where the light is liquid."*

He was recalling one of Rome's magical qualities—its transfixing, liquid light:

We were embracing on the terrace of the Giardino Degli Aranci, a fragrant garden of orange trees on one of Rome's seven hills, a day before I was due to leave for university in England: "Do you really want to give this up?" the girl said as we were looking down at Saint Peter's dome, glowing in the late summer sunset. She meant our relationship, but I heard "Rome"...I had always regarded Rome's ancient stones, its narrow streets, the city's screaming traffic, and blunt, sarcastic people as traveling companions. I was reminded of them in the most unexpected situations: a Mumbai traffic jam, a heated row among Chinese people, an acerbic one-liner from a New Yorker. Rome was still the one I remembered as a kid sauntering on the sampietrinini, *the irregular stones that pave many of the time-torn alleyways. In my mind, I was still the adolescent disappearing into a cloud of dust chasing a football, imploring my friends to pass to me...In other cities, the meeting of lights and stone is often an unhappy one. The warm rays and the cold surface seem to repel one another—a cosmic battle between radiance and matter. Rome's stone is defined by light—the contrast of shadows and bright spots is what gives the city ruins that ethereal, immortal quality.... As I wandered the cobbled alleys, my senses were awakened by the rediscovered light and smells, and I savored feelings I had forgotten. This is Rome, the city I never gave up.*

Francesco and I had a lot in common—we both moved to Rome from our birth cities (he is from Milan), became de-facto Roman citizens, and went to university in London to then pursue careers in international finance, although I became a broker and he a journalist. We both felt the same when it came to what we had left behind but could never truly give up.

I have traveled all over the world and, incidentally, every time I see that magical liquid light which Francesco so eloquently describes, whether it is in Sedona, Arizona, in Luxor, Egypt, or in Bamyan, Afghanistan, my mind and my heart promptly feel at home.

It is, therefore, natural that my cultural heritage presents me with different lenses than those of one of my peers who was born and raised in rural Southwest Missouri or in Bangladesh. I am naturally prone to see life and "reality" through a different set of circumstances. It is the very nature of being human—with time, we all seem to revert to our roots and personal identity, which, at times, might feel lost within the community's identity.

These feelings are shared by many—whether they have been blessed by great opportunities or have lost every possession. I have read many poignant testimonies, very similar to Francesco's, written by Syrians, Palestinians, Iraqis, and Persians. We might not have the same poetic eloquence that Francesco displays, but most of us humans share the same sensitivities and the same needs—we all seek and deserve a home, relationships, memories, and opportunities.

In February 2020, during one of my travels across the Middle East, I experienced two episodes of a very different nature—a television interview and a massage—which reminded me of the unintended consequences of voluntary or involuntary displacement.

On one of the rare schedule breaks, I was watching the Italian news on television and happened to see an interview of a *Giuliano-Dalmata* refugee. The interviewee, a woman, was one of the unfortunate victims of the Istrian-Dalmatian exodus—the post-World War II expulsion and departure of ethnic Italians from the Yugoslav territory of Istria.

Every year, on February 10, Italy commemorates this exodus.

Istria, Rijeka, and Zadar were, for many centuries, ethnically mixed, with long-established Croatian, Italian, and Slovene communities. At the end of World War II, under the Allies' treaty of peace with Italy, the former Italian territories in Istria and Dalmatia were assigned to the new nation of Yugoslavia.

The newly formed Italian republic, which was reeling from the loss of the war and attempting to pacify a very threatening Italian Communist Party, preferred to ignore the plight of the Italian community in Istria and left it to bear the brunt of Josip Broz Tito's policy of ethnic cleansing.

Tito first ordered ethnic Italians to be summarily executed during the beginning of the cleansing campaign, what the Italians call the "foibe massacres," and then he subjected the remaining Italians to other forms of intimidation, such as land expropriation.

This very dignified woman, in her 60s, was being interviewed in her formal drawing room amongst an array of fancy furniture, pictures, and memories. Her expensive Burberry scarf and branded clothing completed the picture of a well-to-do lady. Her testimony was articulate and pragmatic. She managed to stay emotionless even when she recalled her childhood memories, at times full of joy and at times marred by horror, injustice, and unmotivated discrimination. She broke down when she uttered her last phrase on the meaning of being an *esule* (the homeless victim of an exodus): "*...si resta esuli tutta la vita. E le dico di piu'—piu' si cresce, piu'ti senti esule, senza radici. Io ho vissuto bene, ho un marito medico, una famiglia salda... ma saro' sempre un esule. Questa non e' casa mia.*" ("...you'll remain a homeless your entire life. I will tell you more: the more you age, the more you feel homeless, without roots. I have lived well, my husband is a medical doctor, my family is solid... but I will always be homeless. This not my home.")

Take roots away from any human being, and you might cause a loss of identity. This loss leads to disorientation. Disorientation often leads to a desperate search for direction and purpose. This is, in my opinion, when a human being is the most vulnerable. Vulnerability is a dangerous feeling when one cannot come to terms with it. I have faced disoriented foes who were fighting in the hope of defining themselves—they had sought purpose in Jihad while accepting the direction of Islamist doctrines as a defining belief.

The second episode was also quite revealing. After a very physically demanding excursion in *Petra*, Jordan, we decided to indulge ourselves with a massage in the plush surroundings of the Grand Hyatt in *Amman*. The masseuse was a stunning Georgian lady in her late 30s, early 40s. She had moved to Jordan in search of work, had married a local man, and had mothered a child. She had learned to speak Arabic fluently. She felt comfortable to confess that, although she was very appreciative of her host country, she missed her home country terribly, especially her seaside hometown by the Black Sea. She mentioned a Georgian saying: "*When one emigrates to a foreign country and gets his belly full, he starts thinking that he is home, until he grows older and he realizes that his belly and his home are two very different things.*"

I wonder if we might agree that it is easier to place ourselves within a context of values, whether emotional, social, or economic, than to determine where others place themselves.

Most times, we forget that others go through the same exercise as we do. Either consciously or unconsciously, we all go through this measuring-up process, which then influences a decision-making that is mostly aimed at validating individual efforts and achievements.

When I mentor my national security students, I ask them to put themselves in other people's shoes, while abandoning any preconceived opinion of how someone's life should be. This is necessary to fully understand what others may experience and where they place themselves. It is an important tool that my students use when they are entrusted to analyze foreign motives and behaviors. I explain to them that analyzing Qatar's security needs using solely the lenses of experience of a surfer dude from California will help them very little.

Because of this common occurrence, CIA's analysts are constantly warned of the dangers of *mirror-imaging*, as this practice is defined.

Therefore, a common mistake arises when we analyze others using our own value scale. The ability to step out of our persona to define others is among the best skills one can acquire not only as security analysts but also as husbands, wives, fathers, mothers, and work colleagues.

When we operate in a foreign land, we should make sure that we are totally immersed in that culture. I have seen intelligence analysts, journalists, scholars, and policymakers creating pages and pages of literature about a specific nation without ever having visited it. Other times, these people might have worked in the country but never left a base, eaten local foods, or spent any time with locals. As I always tell my students: *"If you get assigned to a Middle Eastern target, make sure that you spend a lot of time in the souk...."*

The leadership culture of the United States military is generally split between senior officers who have been trained to fight big wars against big armies, and those who have been trained to conduct counterinsurgency, asymmetric warfare. Our way of looking at security issues is heavily influenced by the way we were trained. We train the way we fight, and we fight the way we train. My views of security are heavily influenced by the fact that I come from a counterinsurgency background and that I am a Foreign Area Officer, what one would call, in simple terms, the diplomatic corps of the military.

Special Operations Forces (SOF) have developed a cultural-intelligence readiness path to further empower SOF operators and deal effectively with the peculiarities of foreign native environments. The same teachings should also apply to national security analysts and policy makers. In their training, SOF read works by *Bronislaw Malinowsky*, an anthropologist who lived among the natives of the Trobiand Islands in 1918. He maintains that the goal of the foreign affairs experts is *"...to grasp the native's point of view, his relation to life, to realize his vision of the world."*

During a trip to Jordan, I met Sameer Baitamouni, an activist Syrian refugee, who has frequently written against *Bashar al Assad.* It is important to understand that there is a pretty big difference between a Syrian from *Damascus* and a Syrian from *Aleppo*—just as all Italians are not the same. Sameer was kind to share his life and his vision of his world—a world that he felt he had lost:

"I would like to talk about my family history, my family atmosphere related to our roots in Damascus, and my personal experiences between Damascus and Amman.

As we could trace, my family at least is rooted in the eldest inhabited capital in the world and one of the eldest cities in history; we could find names of our family back 280 years. Our reference was based on history books of Damascus that mentioned different figures of the city; one of the family members was part of Omayyad Mosque history.

The whole big family is proud of two martyrs who fought the French army in 1920 around Damascus and were killed in the battle; their names are officially registered.

As well, my grandfather and his brothers and cousins were well known in the old part of the city. The eldest capital, Damascus, has a unique status in the whole region; the more you have roots in the old city, inside the old walls, the more you have heritage. When he died, he left two houses and some shops all in the old part inside the old wall. Actually, that gave us a lot of pride, being rooted inside the old wall of Damascus...

We grew up with temples, Greeks, Romans, Omayyads, Mamluks, Ottomans, and even French history and heritage; this enriched our culture and maybe gave us more pride.

When my father decided to come to Amman to work as he found better income, my mother suffered in the beginning. We came to a smaller city that time, with limited resources, without continuous history like Damascus, which negatively affected the social life, traditions, and habits of the people living in Amman. Bearing in mind that all of the Ammanis were immigrants from different lifestyles left the city without a harmony.

I guess until now, this is a gap the city couldn't adapt to. This might not be clear for outsiders, but for those who know it well, they feel it...

In Damascus, the families of the city shared a lot of small details; they could understand the dress code, the food which is rich, even a lot of daily used words, way of walking, greeting, respect of older people, and more... In Amman, residents immigrated from other countries, other cities, from villages, and some Bedouins, too; the harmony was lost...

I was a boy when my life changed. I could easily integrate into the daily life with others in the school, in the neighborhood, but, at home, my parents were insisting that, one day, we would go back to Damascus, that our stay in Amman wouldn't be much longer... As a family, we used to bring from Damascus (200kms from Amman) our clothes, vegetables, fruits, milk products, Syrian desserts, spices, and more; that gave us the feeling that we were very close to Damascus. Our visits to Damascus during school vacation were a real holiday, a chance to meet aunts, uncles, cousins, and friends, and do some shopping, too.

My personal experience: in my early years in Damascus, I grew up with a big family, on both my father's side or my mother's side, many cousins from different ages, friends, and certain traditions and habits which affected my life then and even now, and forever, too... These traditions were accumulated over hundreds of years: the busy souks, the high sense of humor of the people in the street, the warm greetings for people we don't know, the rooted small handicrafts, the famous kitchen... In Amman, we celebrated big occasions alone; that was painful for the children, who watched friends and neighbors being visited by their families...

In Damascus, I remember that I was surrounded by cousins, aunts, and uncles all the time; this feeling was lost in Amman. My family name had an echo in Damascus, but almost nobody knew about it in Amman... Once I invited a European friend to show her Damascus. I arranged with a tour guide who was 80 years old to meet at the National Museum of Damascus. He started talking to her about my family reputation and some relatives who were active in writing and publishing and other sectors.

She was more proud of me, and she asked me, 'Why I didn't hear this in Amman?' I told her that we don't have roots there...

Another story: the hotel manager was a very-well-educated lady from Damascus. She met with me in private; she spoke good French, and she asked me if I knew a certain lady who owned a first-class school in Damascus. I told her she was my cousin. The lady started telling my friend in French about my family and named some relatives... We were listening in high pride...

Family ties are important in our Mediterranean culture...

Amman is truly a nice city, active and friendly, but it failed to create deep integration for the vast majority of the immigrants, even the first waves. Until now, old and new generations talk about their original cities, towns, villages, and tribes, which we didn't practice in Damascus, and there are no old districts in Amman that we could point to as a reference."

In the 2020 movie *Sergio*, a biopic about the United Nations diplomat Sergio Vieira de Mello, there is a remarkable exchange between the Brazilian diplomat and an East Timorese female refugee, during the UN-sponsored transition in East Timor from a bloody Indonesian occupation to an independent nation. When questioned by de Mello about what she wanted the most for her future, the poor woman, who had been given the opportunity to work in the textile field through UN micro-loans, stated:

"We have been waiting for the future to arrive... if I tell you what I want, I don't think you would understand... My whole life, I worked the land. Today, my land, my family, they are all dead. I don't have anything. You know what I want? I want to go up into the sky and become a cloud. Then travel through the sky to the place where I was born. And when I get there, fall like rain. Then... stay forever... on my soil... on my land. So, let the world see us the way we are. We want to be seen. All of us..."

Sergio Vieira de Mello knew exactly what the woman meant. Although they had come from completely different circumstances, they both carried a hole in their soul. De Mello would die in the 2003 bombing of the UN compound in Baghdad, Iraq—a moment which I will briefly describe later in the book.

There is a popular Neapolitan song about an immigrant who has had to leave everything behind to come to America and search for fortune. Despite having made money, he laments: *"Jo c'aggio perzo a casa patria e onore. Io so' carne 'e maciello so' emigrante"* ("I have lost my home and therefore my honor. I am cannon fodder; I am homeless."). For many, this hole created by identity displacement accompanies them to their final resting place.

John Joseph Gotti, Jr. (1940–2002), the infamous Neapolitan *'capo di tutti i capi,'* who ended up leading the Sicilian Mafia's *Cupola* (leadership council), was the living example of identity displacement, which he attempted to heal by appealing to a code which transcended family ties and centered on warrior criminal masculinity.

At the end of his life, during a conversation with his son, Gotti showed the same lack of repentance that I would later witness in many Islamists. He was said to have stated: *"...what family are you talking about? Are you talking about your four hundred brothers, cousins, and uncles? Being a man is not being a guy who is looking for closure. My freedom and my life take a back seat to my duty and manhood. These are my standards. I don't run; I don't hide in shadows..."*

So, it might then be a Mafia boss and not a Jihadist who first provided me with the most valuable insight regarding murderous absolutisms—criminal fundamentalism is not an ideology; it is a mindset.

Similarly, terrorism is not an ideology. It is a tactic—an often-criminal tactic—whether it is adopted by a criminal organization or by a jihadist movement. That is the reason I believe that the term *Global War on Terrorism* (GWOT) might be misunderstood by many—a war to end a tactic? GWOT is a brand and not a campaign, or a strategy. GWOT analysis cannot be a tool to understand the nature of the Middle Eastern cultural identity and the reasons for identity displacement. Terrorism is a tactical response caused by the damaging effects of cultural and identity displacement. It is not a cause; it is a consequence. This very common misunderstanding arises, for example, through the Israeli narrative that Palestinians are being displaced because they support acts of terrorism. I argue that it is exactly the opposite: when people are displaced, they can develop a fundamentalist mindset which, according to circumstances, might force them to embrace terrorist tactics. History is full of records of Jewish terrorism, caused by displacement, from the times of resistance against Roman occupation, to the origins of the creation of the modern State of Israel. Israelis know better.

To avoid unnecessary misunderstandings, there are other, more appropriate factors to consider when we look at identity and identity displacement in the Middle East.

One of these factors I like to define as the mythical quality of Middle Eastern identity: in the land of *"One Thousand and One Nights,"* myths are vital. Land and landmarks make myth real and validate a people and its heritage.

To semi-nomadic tribes, fallen powers, or displaced people, stories of their ancestors can be as vital as food and water. The mythological landscape of the Middle East is ever present in the stories of people who commonly claim that one of their ancestors had participated in a particular battle which occurred four centuries earlier, or in the constant claims of ancient injustice which permeate the Holy Land— the land of grief and miracles. Middle Eastern identity resides in its mythological landscape, and its myths have a very sophisticated quality.

Landmarks are vital for Arabs and Muslims. More than once, I was called a *Nasrani* by Arabs—a *Nazarene*. I was not born in Nazareth, but I am a Christian. Therefore, the landmark that is, for all Arabs, Jesus' birthplace, defines me in their eyes.

Amos Rapoport, an Australian architect and anthropologist, stated that a tribe's cherished myths—of its origin, its meaning, its purpose in the world—are unobservable realities constantly seeking expression in observable reality.

In the book *The Road to Ubar,* by *Nicholas Clapp,* it describes how Southern Arabia, for example, has three important tiers of mythological landscape—the sites of roaming Bedouins' legendary raids and battles, the sites where *Djinns* (evil spirits/creatures) reside, and the holy sites of Islam's patriarchs and prophets.

In other words, mess with the physical landscape, unilaterally set borders, or build walls, and you shall affect identity.

In the same book, it explains that the Arabic identity is also very connected with historical trade and economic balance. The economy of frankincense and its dramatic effect on the region are frequently brought up as an example of how trade has shaped the geo-cultural landscape of the Middle East.

In other words, mess with opportunities and the historic economic landscape, and you will affect identity.

I once had the pleasure to dine with *David Price Williams,* the renowned Welsh archaeologist with very prominent experience in the Middle East and specifically in the Holy Land. Dave has a degree in Ancient Near Eastern languages and Classical Greek and a doctorate in Near Eastern archaeology, and has spent his working life as an East Mediterranean archaeologist. His first overseas field work was, in 1969, as a surveyor at the classical site of *Knidos* in Turkey. He then worked for the Smithsonian Institution before directing his own field research in the same area through the 1970s. He is a Fellow of the Royal Geographical Society and an elected life member of the Society for Old Testament Studies.

In the incredible setting of the Panorama Restaurant, overlooking the lights of Luxor, I asked David, point-blank, the same question that I ask almost every Middle East expert I meet: What was, in his opinion, the most relevant moment in the history of the modern Middle East?

Without missing a beat, his answer was: *"Easily, the Sykes-Picot agreement and the creation of the State of Israel. Centuries of historical tolerance and regional and individual identities were destroyed by these two acts."*

An act of colonial domination, the Sykes-Picot was a secret World War I agreement between Britain and France laying out zones of influence through the forced partitioning of Mesopotamia and the Levant. Control of these lands was to be taken from Turkey if the Ottomans lost the war.

The vast majority of Middle Easterners would promptly agree with Dave. Whether the disastrous consequences of that fateful secret agreement were intentional or not, the damage was done.

In addition to the popular belief in the political and strategic short-sightedness of the Sykes-Picot partitions and of the creation of the State of Israel, we might add the unique nature of the three major religions of the Middle East, which definitely do not make things easier.

As a Roman Catholic, I would be the first to admit that Abrahamic religions might have a theology brimming with trust, but they have a heart full of suspicion—maybe just as a result of history.

Sometimes, the damage to cultural identity and heritage is completely intentional.

During a trip to Egypt, I had the pleasure to meet *Abdel Hamid Salah el Sharief,* who is the chairman of the Smithsonian Cultural Rescue Initiative. This organization's mission is "to protect cultural heritage threatened or impacted by disasters and to help U.S. and international communities preserve their identities and history."

In other words, Mr. Salah heads *The Monuments Men* of the Middle East. He was the one who introduced me to the concept that "home" is the combination of three vital factors: relationships, memories, and opportunities.

Abdel Hamid, who is Egyptian, maintains that cultural heritage in the Middle East is primarily about memories/stories/myths that go from generation to generation. It is about values and message. The physical sites are important because they are validations of these stories.

In *Mosul,* ISIS (The Caliphate) destroyed more than 90 percent of the city's cultural heritage. The Caliphate's strategy, according to

Abdel Hamid, was to destroy the historical evidence of the area's multi-cultural and religious tolerance and successful amalgamation. The Caliphate attempted to validate its absolutist fundamentalism and its divisive view of the world by destroying any proof of multi-cultural and interreligious ecumenical success.

Interestingly, Abdel Hamid stated that Sunni Iraqis had flocked to the mirage of The Caliphate to find their lost identity "*because they are broken, rootless people.*" Saddam Hussein had intentionally erased all prior cultural history to establish the cult in his own person and in the attempt to force socialist *Ba'athist* doctrine on a fiercely independent tribal society.

It is now believed that, once the West removed Saddam Hussein, millions of orphans were automatically created by Ambassador Paul Bremer's final *coup de grace*.

Lewis Paul Bremer III led the Coalition Provisional Authority (CPA) in Iraq, from May 2003 until June 2004. The CPA was created to normalize the country, after the 2003 invasion that toppled Saddam Hussein. As the top civilian administrator, Bremer was permitted to rule by decree. With the first two decrees, Bremer managed to take out the two strongest pillars of Iraqi identity under Saddam Hussein. His first decree banned the Ba'ath party in all forms, and the second dismantled the Iraqi Army. Bremer's first two decisions, as a foreigner, were to dismantle Iraq's two largest employment pools.

Abdel Hamid also felt that the same might be happening to post-*Muammar al-Gaddafi's* Libya and post-*Yahya bin Muhammad Hamid ad-Din* and *Ahmad bin Yahya's* Yemen.

So, why do "orphaned" people flock to radical ideas in search of identity?

The first underlying reason is the combination of the individual desire for emotional connection, which may lead to individuals being influenced by others, whether it's due to charisma or a lack of knowledge on the individual's part, and the natural, often irrational, response swayed by emotions. Natural, because human beings by nature are not rational and have a propensity to seek prompt solutions as their needs and wants arise.

The second reason is that, as we are swept by emotions and we are irrational creatures, we tend to fall into affiliations which might cause a herd mentality. This is part of our need to belong to not only a herd but to a tribe or a community of beliefs, which is why a single good orator can sway public opinion one way or the other.

For example, during the *ventennio fascista*—the span of 20 years in which Benito Mussolini had grasped the arduous reality of creating a new national identity out of a very complicated cultural mosaic—he had taken over a country where many regional identities experienced a constant struggle between the needs for autonomy versus security and the fear of abandonment versus entrapment. So, he invented Fascism. The word comes from the Latin word *fascis*, which means "bundle". It is a Roman symbol of power consisting of a bound bundle of wooden rods, sometimes including an axe with its blade emerging. Mussolini's *fascist* attempt at unity through martial strength was an anachronistic Neo-Roman imperial experiment, aimed at unifying all these different interests into a collective need. It failed spectacularly.

Equally as spectacularly, other attempts at repeating glorious past history have failed to yield the original realities they sought to emulate: Adolph Hitler and his Third Reich, Mussolini and his neo-Roman empire, Gamal Abdel Nasser and his Pan-Arabist dream, Mohammad Reza Pahlavi and his neo-imperial Iran, Abu Bakr al Baghdadi and his Islamic Caliphate dream, to name a few.

Fortunately, ethnic communities continue to thrive, even more cemented in their traditions and pride, on the ruins of these failed political experiments, providing that their ancestral homes have survived. A fitting example is the resilience of tribal structure in the Iraqi province of Al Anbar, a reality that I will address in the next chapter.

 # Killing the Caliphate

> "Then Yeshua said to him, Return the
> sword to its place, for all of those who
> take up swords will die by swords."
> New Testament—Matthew 26:52

> "There is a time for everything, and a season
> for every activity under the heavens: a time
> to be born and a time to die, a time to plant
> and a time to uproot, a time to kill and a
> time to heal, a time to tear down and a time
> to build ... a time to love and a time to hate,
> a time for war and a time for peace."
> Old Testament—Ecclesiastes 3

I HAD WITNESSED IRAQ in the aftermath of toppling Saddam Hussein when I operated in the predominantly Shia province of *Dhi-Qar*. I served with the *Corpo Militare della Croce Rossa Italiana (CRIMIL)*, the military unit of the Italian Red Cross, which, as an auxiliary component of the Italian armed forces, has rendered civil-affairs capacity (refugee assistance, prisoners-of-war processing, humanitarian disaster relief, and vital medical support) in every conflict since the Italian unification.

As I mentioned in the preface of the book, when it comes to the Middle East, and, in this case, Iraq, we need to challenge our understanding of "end-state", as we are in no position, so early in the game, to correctly define what an end-state in Iraq looks like. Seventeen years since the 2003 invasion is still a very early stage.

The first glaring example of the importance of time and end-state was offered to me, during my second tour in Iraq, as I was eating in the Italian military cafeteria at *Camp Mittica*. As I looked to my right, I saw five British *Desert Rats* personnel happily sharing a meal with their Italian *Ariete Brigade* colleagues. It was 2006. Between the 23rd of October and the 11th of November 1942, these two military units had slaughtered each other, during the battle of El Alamein, on the Libyan-Egyptian border.

Sixty-four years later, they would be fighting on the same side and happily sharing meals. I am safe to assume that, 64 years before witnessing that lunch at *Camp Mittica*, both the Italian and British War Cabinets would had envisaged very different end-states.

Most sociologists point to the common Christian background of the European countries as the element for the relatively rapid appeasement—an element which would be missing in the Middle East. I am not sure that theory is completely accurate.

In 2006, although we were initially welcomed as liberators by the *Shia* population, we were still *Nazarene* outsiders and had to tread very carefully to avoid unnecessary intromissions into the local sectarian dynamics and the Iraqi way of doing business. The Shia population of South Iraq was, on average, very grateful for our help in getting rid of Saddam Hussein, but it was also very clear that we should know our place and avoid intruding in something we had no business tampering with.

The signs of Saddam's attempt at cleansing the identity of the Shia South were still vivid in the dry marshes and the memories of the atrocious punishments that Saddam had imparted on the local tribal leadership, in the aftermath of the Allied war to liberate Kuwait, in 1991. Encouraged by how quickly we had routed the mighty Iraqi Army, the Shia of southern Iraq had rebelled against Saddam but were promptly crushed. The painful memories were still very recent.

The Shia, who felt that they had been abandoned by the West, did not ultimately trust us.

Therefore, we had no business questioning what had occurred or interfering with the desires of revenge. Tribal leadership and identity—whether Sunni or Shia—although weakened by Saddam's efforts, was still very strong and clearly constituted the primary guarantee of much-needed safety and continuity in Iraq.

This time around, we might have finally been the liberators, but we were merely accepted as providers of services to cater for the dire physiological needs of the Iraqi population—medical, food, water, sanitation.

Every service we offered had to go through the approval of the local leaders. Our material support had to be seen as primarily coming through the intercession of a local chieftain. He was given the credit for successfully negotiating on behalf of his community. We were forced to legitimize the local power structure. Any attempt at circumventing this practice was met with force.

In 2003, foreign troops were being warned, all over the country, as non-American targets were being hit as a stark reminder that we were no longer being perceived as liberators but increasingly as occupiers. In Baghdad, the Jordanian and Turkish embassies, Sergio Vieira de Mello's United Nations compound, and the headquarters of International Committee of the Red Cross had been attacked.

On 12 November 2003, in Nasiriyah, the *Carabinieri's* (Italian Military Police) *Maestrale* base was hit by suicide bombers, causing the single largest loss of Italian military personnel since the end of World War II.

The attack was a hammer blow to the Italian psyche. The emotional scars of World War II are still very present in a country that, as mentioned, has the second-oldest population in the world.

In the aftermath of that devastating conflict, Italians had crafted a Constitution in which the repudiation of war as *"an instrument of offense against the freedom of other peoples and as a mean of resolving international disputes…*" has constituted the moral underpinning by which, every single time Italian troops had to be deployed outside the national borders, it would have to be exclusively in support of peacekeeping missions.

The *Maestrale* attack destroyed that fragile *"missione di pace"* (peacekeeping mission) veneer as the bloodshed of war came back into Italian homes. I was in shock. Two weeks later, I called a CRIMIL recruiter, re-enlisted, and went to Iraq to do my part.

Ten years later, I experienced another pivotal moment but, this time, as a reserve United States Navy Foreign Area Officer.

My experience in dealing with the Islamic State of Syria and the Levant (The Caliphate) started in 2015, when I was asked to augment the Combined Joint Interagency Task Force—Syria (CJIATF-S), and ended in 2019, with the complete defeat of the physical Caliphate.

By 2015, I had already been in the combat zones of Iraq and Afghanistan several times. I had developed an opinion on the nature of conflict, in general. This next four-year experience would finally shape my views of war and its underlying reasons.

Most of the information about the CJIATF-S operation is still classified. This task force was created, by order of the Obama administration, to manage the $500 million emergency fund allocated to train and equip *"moderate and vetted"* Syrian rebels who could counteract the rapid advance of The Caliphate, in Syria.

Large swaths of Iraq, north of its capital, Baghdad, had already been lost to this violent phenomenon. Our Kurdish allies in Northern Iraq and across the Iraqi/Syrian border were hanging on by a thread. What would have happened if this fundamentalist Sunni movement had taken over the entirety of Syria? What of neighboring Israel? Even Shia Iran did not seem capable of stemming the swelling of The Caliphate's ranks and its rapid advances.

Conscious of the risks of doing nothing but cautious about replicating another "surge" into Iraq, the Obama administration requested emergency funding to enable local fighters to counteract the threat and appointed a very capable U.S. Army officer to lead the charge, Major General *Michael Nagata*—a U.S. Special Forces operator.

Working for Nagata was, for me, the equivalent of a master's degree in international relations. It is amazing to see, in practice, how a leader must balance tactical savvy with diplomatic skill. Considering how complex and daunting the task was from the beginning, Nagata was a flawless and excellent teacher.

The problems he had to face were clear from the start—a difficulty establishing what *"moderate"* means when you compare Western and Middle Eastern standards: the uncertainty of the military strategy and the sheer number of stakeholders pitching in to define vetting measures. I counted 22 "interested" Western and Middle Eastern parties between agencies, militaries, and governments. The Caliphate was a threat to many, although the intensity of that threat greatly varied, depending on which party you would consider. Nagata's cool under political fire was legendary.

After the invaluable learning experience at CJIATF-S, I went on to serve under another great military leader who shared the same commitment to diplomacy that Nagata had displayed. This time, I augmented the *Operation Inherent Resolve* (OIR) mission.

On 17 October 2014, the Department of Defense had formally established *Combined Joint Task Force—Operation Inherent Resolve* (CJTF-OIR) in order to formalize ongoing military actions against The Caliphate. This designation established the first operational headquarters on Iraqi soil since the departure of American troops from the region in 2011.

The month before, a *Global Coalition to Defeat ISIS/Da'esh* had been founded. It was based on worldwide concern for the threat that The Caliphate posed to international peace and security. The U.S.-convened coalition eventually consisted of 87 members, including Iraq, 81 foreign nations, and 5 international organizations: the Arab League, the Community of Sahel-Saharan States, the European Union, Interpol, and NATO.

CJTF-OIR was designed to be Iraq's primary military partner in the war against The Caliphate. It was a U.S.-led mission that included 15 other countries—Australia, Britain, Canada, Denmark, France, Germany, Italy, Jordan, Morocco, the Netherlands, Norway, Portugal, Spain, Sweden, and Turkey.

Some of these countries deployed a consistent number of "boots on the ground" in addition to considerable naval and air assets. It is an historical certainty that the support of the international coalition and the sacrifice of the Iraqi and Syrian militaries, as well as that of the anti-Caliphate forces, were the reasons for the destruction of the physical Caliphate.

From 2017 to 2019, I served as a Foreign Area Officer negotiating and coordinating the force generation and the international coalition's contributions to the D-ISIS campaign. My "clients" were a number of foreign armed forces and governments. The military mission to eliminate The Caliphate, its geographical significance, and its military capacity was an undeniable success.

It is undoubtable that the victory was achieved primarily in conjunction with indigenous partner forces. The result of the campaign met the initial official CJTF-OIR strategic objective:

"The Coalition strategy acknowledges that the best forces to win the fight against ISIS are local forces. In Iraq, we are partnered with the Iraqi security forces, which includes the Iraqi army, the Iraqi air force, the Counter Terrorism Service, the Federal Police, and the Kurdish Peshmerga. In Syria, the Coalition is partnered with the Syrian Democratic Forces and their partner Syrian Arab Coalition, who are focused on fighting ISIS. Ultimately, the military victory over ISIS will be accomplished by the indigenous forces; we will accomplish our mission with those indigenous forces, and improved regional stability will be attained through those partners."

This strategic definition was reflected in my commander's vision of how to conduct this kind of military operations. *Joseph Leonard Votel*, a U.S. Army Ranger, was not only a superb military commander but also a very decent human being and a seasoned diplomat who always sought a deep understanding of a conflict's socio-cultural aspects.

Votel was a proponent of the "By-With-Through" approach, which is based on the operational belief that regional conflicts can be resolved only with the full, primary participation of local actors.

In an interview for the military publication *Joint Forces Quarterly*, Votel explained his view of the By-With-Through approach:

"One of the key things we've learned about By, With, and Through is that he who owns the effects owns the impact these operations generate. What we strive to do through this approach is to keep the ownership of the problem, and its aftermath, with the affected people. In Iraq, it's the Iraqi Security Forces, and in Syria, it's the Syrian Democratic Forces [SDF]. In many ways, that's the more burdensome aspect of military operations. How do we transition to local governance, local security for consolidation, stability, and reconstruction? The earlier we can get the local or host-nation forces involved, the better. That's really key.... One of the things we have to understand is that locals call the shots...."

The craft consisted in understanding which locals had to be supported to call the shots. In Iraq, where the Caliphate had started its advance, we could not afford to repeat the very mistakes that had contributed to an environment in which The Caliphate had been allowed to originate and prosper.

Shia and Kurdish forces were the obvious parties for us to consider in the fight against The Caliphate, but the risk of disenfranchising again the Sunni tribes, some of which were now the bedrock of The Caliphate, had to be mitigated.

A 2014 study by *Patricio Asura-Heim* for *CNA Analysis and Solutions*, titled *"No Security Without Us—Tribes and Tribalism in Al Anbar Province, Iraq"* should be compulsory training material for fighters, peacekeepers, civil-affairs and foreign-area officers, and policy makers who have to work on Iraq.

The study was completed in the early stage of the fight against The Caliphate and suggested that: *"Luckily, the ISIS-led insurgency is by no means monolithic. Reminiscent of Al Qaeda's rise in Iraq beginning in 2003, the ISIS campaign is currently supported by a host of actors, ranging from former Ba'athists to disaffected Sunni tribes at odds with a sectarian Shia government and its exclusionary policies. These alliances are born of convenience and a shared hatred of the current government of Iraq. But given the bloody history between Islamic extremists and Al Anbar's tribes, each must be eyeing the other warily. As was the case during the years of heavy American presence in Iraq, a key to security going forward will be to peel away moderate Sunni tribes from the insurgency, turn them against the terrorists, and begin a legitimate national reconciliation process between Iraq's Sunni, Shia, and Kurdish populations. While the path to enduring stability in Iraq involves effective national-level political accommodations, the task at hand is to extirpate ISIS to create space for negotiations among Iraq's various political and ethnic factions. Doing so will require partnering with local tribal forces in Sunni areas…"*

The study goes on to describe in detail the historical and cultural origins of modern tribalism in the area. It explains, for example, how tribes like the *Albu Risha* and *Albu Mahal* had gone from being the nomadic military mini-states that had supported T. E. Lawrence (Lawrence of Arabia, the legendary British officer) in the fight against the Turks during World War I, to urbanized powerhouses after supporting the U.S. counterinsurgency fight against al Qaeda, in 2006–2007.

"Nomadic tribes rooted in pastoralism, commerce, and conquest have been replaced by settled village or city communities, mainly along the Euphrates River from Fallujah to Al Qaim, consisting of extended families or clans. Today's contemporary rural-urban hybrids are held together by traditional tribal characteristics of solidarity (asabiyya), true (and more-often fictitious) kinship ties, patron-client relationships, and tribal customs and laws. Although traditional tribal organization is disappearing in the urban setting, modern tribes maintain elements of tribal culture and retain the ability to mobilize politically and militarily. In modern Iraq, tribalism lives in symbiosis with contemporary ideologies and social and political movements."

The gem of the study is the very useful terminology guide and the extensive explanation of tribal traditions, which regulate allegiance, kinship, and behavioral etiquette.

In the vast, desertic expanse of northwestern Iraq, the Anbari tribal alliance has been the surviving identity structure that has grown stronger by providing protection, access to economic resources, and a means for obtaining justice to the post-Saddam "orphans" during what came to be known to Iraqis as the *White Governorate*—the Allied occupation.

Asfura-Heim describes tribal values and social norms by quoting historian Phebe Marr: *"Among the legacies of (Bedouin) tribalism in Iraq are the intense preoccupations with family, clan, and tribe; devotion to personal honor; factionalism; and above all, difficulty in cooperation across kinship lines."*

He asserts that: *"Perhaps the most fundamental implication of tribalism is the strong sense of group identity and subordination of individual interests to those of the group. Tribesmen believe that their individual destinies depend on the character of their lineage and how it is perceived by members of other lineages. The Bedouins' view is that a good and honorable life is possible only within the confines of one's own tribal people and that, therefore, refuge seekers, or muzabin, 'are constantly tasting balash,' or social death."*

To a Sunni *Bedu* from Northwestern Iraq, *arain* or *harem* is "home." It is both a sanctuary and the very concept that gives the Bedu meaning. He will protect it with his life. The alternative is *ayb*—"shame," or, even worse, *balash*, once he has become a *muzabin*.

Muzabin are refuge seekers, displaced people who could not defend their home. *Balash* is the loss of honor and status, the social death suffered by refuge seekers who are no longer able to live in their tribal home.

Disenfranchise, or, worse, displace one of these people, and you have a war on your hands.

As my passion has always been history, I feel extremely privileged to have been a front-seat spectator in the historic event which was the destruction of the physical Caliphate. I was able to be a part of it from the initial coalition's ground advances through the epic and bloody door-to door-liberation of *Mosul* in July 2017, the taking of *Raqqa,* barely three months later, and finally, the surreal last stand of the few remaining Caliphate fighters and their families on the dusty terrain of the *Jabal Baghuz.*

I could not stop making mental comparisons with the battles that I had studied. Seeing the terrified looks on ISIS prisoners, I could not help but wonder if it had been the same for the crusaders at *Hattin,* the Roman legionnaires of the *Fulminata* at *Beit Horon,* or the British Redcoats at *Maiwand.* What do despair and terror look like?

There was a difference, though: it was in how the surviving ISIS fighters and their families were treated when we closed in on them, and they chose to become *muzabin* by giving up their cause in exchange for their lives to be spared. We made a conscientious effort to show that we were different from them.

Had the Kurdish fighters and our Special Forces operators been the Jewish rebels who had faced the Romans in 66 AD, or the Afghan warriors who had faced the British Redcoats in 1880, there would be no Caliphate survivors, not even women and children.

Had the Kurdish fighters and our Special Forces operators been ISIS fighters, there would have been no ISIS survivors.

After seeing the inevitable revenges perpetrated by the Iraqi Security Forces after the liberation of Mosul and northern Iraq, I felt proud of the humane treatment that had been reserved for the remaining thousands of Caliphate fighters, women, and children who, without food or a roof over their heads, were huddling together in the bitter cold of a 500-yard-wide area. That is what being hopelessly surrounded looks like. I had witnessed, firsthand, one of the many Middle Eastern checkmates.

What bothered me to no end were not the defeated and stunned blank stares of the once-proud Caliphate fighters but the disrespectful defiance of the women. While they were being transported (and I emphasize *transported,* not *marched*) with their children, to the relative safety of refugee camps like *Al-Hawl,* they were still chanting Caliphate slogans with their hatred-filled scowls. Some were even encouraging their children to remember our faces and to exact revenge in the future—a final act of defiance to mask the painful loss of everything they stood for. But why?

While the captured fighters still languish in Kurdish prisons, their wives and the many ISIS widows have created a mini-Caliphate in the refugee camps. Camp guards do not dare to go inside the 12,000-person-strong foreign section of the Al-Hawl camp. That section has been aptly renamed *Jabal Baghuz* by the Caliphate women as an additional act of defiance. Again, why?

The essence of defiance is described in the opening scene of the movie *Gladiator,* directed by *Ridley Scott.* The Roman legions are squaring off against the Germanics in what is looming to be a bloody and unequal confrontation. The Germanics refuse an offer to surrender and start a war "haka" intended to rally their own spirits and to intimidate the enemy. The Romans stand in line, unfazed, as they had faced hundreds of these shows. They are just preoccupied with readying their well-practiced killing machine. *Quintus,* one of the Roman senior officers, states: *"People should know when they are conquered."* *Maximus,* his commander, promptly retorts: *"Would you, Quintus? Would I?"*

When certain of our own beliefs and righteousness, would any of us shrink in the face of what we perceive to be an injustice?

Roman legionnaires, Germanic warriors, and these Caliphate women might have had a lot in common when it came to motivation: they were all fighting for honor and over land, which, for different reasons, they claimed was rightfully theirs. *"Vis honorque"* would say the Romans—*"strength and honor"*—or, even more appropriately, *"honor through force."* I could relate to that. You have lost your land, you have lost your dream, and you feel your honor has evaporated with it. What have you got left? Is life still worth living?

However, whether brainwashed, true believers, or hopeless orphans, I still could not find sympathy for these women. There was no honor in their fight, there was no respect for the enemy—no compassion, just hate, pure hate, and a belief that we were not even human beings; this is what they had no problem reminding us. Their breed were children to be loved and protected while the child of a Yazidi woman was an easily expendable, useless mouth to feed. How could they think like this? They were mothers, too, after all.

I had to deal with extreme paradoxes, especially when it came to Belgian ISIS brides—an episode that I will recount later.

But above all, it was the ruthless actions and selfish double standards, from not only women who had grown up accustomed to violence but from girls who had been born and raised in the comfortable environments of middle-class European families, that filled me with rage. *Should they be treated like they would have treated Yazidi and Christian women, and children?* I kept asking myself.

The United States Central Command and my own personal beliefs provided the answer: Justice is about creating and upholding order. It is not about satiating anger. It is about finding a balance. The punishment, at times, cannot be proportionate, because, if it is aimed at retribution rather than seeking order, it ensures long-lasting strife and perennial bloodshed. *In media stat virtus.* Virtue resides in the middle ground. Ultimate peace can only be achieved with authentic, impartial righteousness. The Caliphate was ultimately doomed from the beginning because it had failed to embrace this basic historical reality. It had chosen to focus on the wrong historical narrative. We could not repeat ISIS' mistake.

During my four-year service to defeat The Caliphate, I had continuously tried to make sense of the horrors that had been perpetrated, initially by The Caliphate, and then as the initial resulting backlash, by its Iraqi, Iranian, and Syrian opponents.

There is no doubt in my mind that, although motivated by plausible ideals based on a common identifier, the recruiting methods of The Caliphate were deceiving and criminal. Its warfare and justice methods were cruel and, again, criminal. The Caliphate, from its leadership to its foot soldiers, acted criminally and preyed on the weakest with unjustified cunning and immense brutality. The Caliphate deserved its end *"for all of those who take up swords will die by swords."*

One of The Caliphate's manuals is *The Management of Savagery: The Most Critical Stage Through Which the Umma Will Pass*, by *Abu Bakr Naji*. In this book, the word "fear" is very frequently used both as a term of reference and as a psychological warfare tool:

"Likewise, it is suitable for groups that want to send a message to the enemy that waves of fear and paying the price for its actions will never end…. The enemy may do whatever it wishes with the Muslim masses; rather, we are preparing for another wave of operations which will fill their hearts with fear, and this fear will have no end… By doing so, the amount of the enemy's fear is multiplied, and good media goals are achieved… The policy of violence must also be followed such that, if the demands are not met, the hostages should be liquidated in a terrifying manner, which will send fear into the hearts of the enemy and his supporters… Power (al-shawka) is achieved through ties of religious loyalty (bil-muwallah al-imaniyya). When the enemy knows that if he breaks a portion of a group, the remainder will capitulate, we are able to say that this group has not achieved 'power.' But if the enemy knows that, if he kills a portion of the group, vengeance for their blood will be undertaken by the remainder and that the targets of the group will stay in place until they have destroyed the last of them, that group has achieved 'power' which the enemy fears, especially if the organization of the group is hard to destroy in a single strike…"

The deliberate use of horror, the gruesome killing, the crucifixions, the beheadings and raping of innocents, the broadcasting of these criminal actions on social media, was not only the result of socio-pathological behavior but also an intentional plan to instill fear in their opponents so that little to no resistance would be offered to counter the advance of The Caliphate. Although this has been a traditional Muslim tactic since the initial Islamic conquests of 700 AD, we can find the same tactics in other areas, irrespective of religious identity, such as in the case of Mexican narco-traffickers. The scenes of skinned-alive and decapitated people being hung from bridges has been as common in Ciudad Juarez as in Mosul.

Initially, what I could not make sense of was why so many people from all over the world had flocked to swell The Caliphate's ranks, were bought into its beliefs, and chose to die rather than return to their countries of origin. Why would an Australian, a British, or an American kid prefer to be slaughtered in the middle of a very foreign country, thousands of miles away from his own family, rather than stay close to those he loved?

In August 2017, *Graeme Wood*, an American journalist, penned the article *"True Believers: How ISIS Made Jihad Religious Again"* for *Foreign Affairs* magazine, in which he reviewed the book *Anatomy of Terror: From the Death of Bin Laden to the Rise of the Islamic State,* by *Ali Soufan*, a Lebanese-American former FBI agent who worked on a number of high-profile anti-terrorism cases. The following are some important excerpts from Wood's analysis:

"On September 11, 2001, Al Qaeda commanded an army of 400. A decade and a half later, the Islamic State (or ISIS) had mobilized some 40,000 people to travel to Iraq and Syria, mostly from the Muslim-majority countries but also from Western countries with sizable Muslim communities and even from places with relatively few Muslims, such as Chile and Japan... If anything, the figure of 40,000 understates the proliferation of jihad. It does not include the thousands loyal to the Taliban, or the tens of thousands of violent extremists in North Africa, Southeast Asia, and the Caucasus. Nor does it include people who would have traveled to Iraq or Syria to join ISIS if their home

governments hadn't made such trips illegal or impossible. Meanwhile, the 40,000-person figure does include noncombatants—which actually makes it a more impressive indicator of the group's appeal. Young men can be counted on to show up in large numbers for just about any war, but a violent cause that inspires elderly people and women—including some who are pregnant or caring for young children—must be doing something special... "*But what looked like the runt of the Al Qaeda litter was, in fact, another species altogether. ISIS asked its followers to join not because it was fighting U.S. troops—an orthodox bin Ladenist goal—but because it had established the world's only Islamic state, with no law but God's, and with a purity of purpose that even the Taliban had not envisioned. Tens of thousands of people did not cross continents and seas to fight for a third-string Al Qaeda franchise. They came to fight for a kingdom of heaven on earth.*"

Differing from my belief that religion was merely a banner and the necessary opiate to create the unifying identity for the otherwise-religious-illiterate recruits, Wood sees a distinct theological motivator behind The Caliphate: "*...BBC's Quentin Sommerville and Riam Dalati published a moving multimedia piece that reconstructed the lives of a few ISIS fighters whose corpses had been found, rotting and picked over by dogs, on the shore of the Tigris River near Mosul, Iraq. The photographs on the mobile phone of one of the fighters revealed details of their training and their personal lives. They were barely men. Their beards were wispy and their recreations adolescent. They smiled and joked with friends. The religious side of their existence was evident: they followed their imam; they memorized Scripture; they aspired to die in the path of God... ISIS is religious first and political second; it is public, nonexclusive, and religiously uncompromising. No explanation of the past decade's jihadist Great Awakening makes sense without taking into account that contrast.*"

A 2017 essay for the *New England Journal of Public Policy*, titled "Understanding the ISIS Appeal" and penned by *Lydia Watson* of the University of Oxford, is a very detailed analysis of the methods and motivators behind ISIS recruiting. It is also a very meaningful summary of the cultural and social reasons behind the wave of interested *jihadis*.

Watson writes: *"Western media have done a good job of publicizing the brutal side of ISIS: the videos, photos, and statements that ISIS has issued showing beheadings of westerners, the mass executions of Shia soldiers, and the statements of threats to any kuffars, or unbelievers...This dissemination has spread fear of the group in the West, one of ISIS's aims. but it has also obscured to a Western audience the revolutionary message of idealism and joy that attracts many young people to the cause, which, in turn, blocks our understanding of and our ability to combat the appeal.*

It all adds up, however, to a rather simple message: for the first time in a hundred years there is a caliphate, an Islamic state, but, unlike that of the Ottomans, it is truly following God's law, strictly, with no corruption. This difference makes the caliphate a utopia on Earth, and for some people, this utopia will usher in the apocalypse following the defeat of the kuffar armies inevitably ranged against it, and it is every Muslim's duty to travel there... and help build this fledgling state."

For Watson, as for Woods, the religious appeal is the lynchpin to the attraction which cements the beauty of identifying with a large, homogenous group. An *Umma* (the Islamic Community), which, although coming from different parts of the world and belonging to different races, transcends the imaginary barriers created by geography, economic conditions, and social injustice and comes together to join God's paradise on Earth. Watson observes that The Caliphate's utopic media production showed *"...all generations (boys and girls and men of all ages but no women) and a range of races (one mujatweet features only happy, blond Bosnian children); they stress the camaraderie and joy of living in a utopia, and they show a land of plenty, where the markets are full of fresh produce and the meals are generous, and where children in the park are handed candy floss and chocolate by smiling fighters. There is even a mujatweet profiling a shawarma seller. The fight, however, is never sidelined: guns are omnipresent, with most featured men clearly fighters, even when children are profiled...*

There is no mistaking the message that the next generation of the Islamic State is made up of diverse, happy, committed, and militant citizens. The narrative not only attracts idealistic young Muslims, but it helps encourage people already in the Islamic State who are discouraged by the hardships they encounter: the lack of electricity, Western luxuries, sometimes food and basic medical supplies, and, in some areas, the constant bombardment. Of course, it is hard, the narrative tells them, because this is the beginning; everything new must be built with sacrifice and effort. The brutality of the ISIS interpretation of sharia, when witnessed in person, can be a shock, but this, too, can be overcome, ISIS argues, using the narrative of a new state: once people are used to the law, there will be less crime and thus, inevitably, less need to punish people. In other words, these are just birthing pains."

In September 2017, *Jytte Clausen*, a Danish professor of International Cooperation at Brandeis University and a local affiliate at the Center for European Studies at Harvard University, penned a review of the book *Terror in France: The Rise of Jihad in the West,* by French political scientist *Gilles Kepel,* again for *Foreign Affairs* magazine.

This review, which was titled *"Terror in the Terroir: The Roots of France's Jihadist Problem"* is very important because Kepel is very close to French President Macron and because France has been a major source of Muslim youth who volunteered as cannon fodder for Islamist causes. Kepel blames Islamist fundamentalism for the ever-present terrorist threat in his country threat but sees it as just one part of a larger rise in identity politics.

"In his view, this broader trend (of French citizens flocking to The Caliphate's cause) *presents a profound threat to French society, as it is incompatible with traditional French ideals. ...Kepel offers an impassioned indictment of religious and nationalist extremism in French politics... Kepel identifies two main causes of the jihadist surge in France: the Internet and the emergence of ethno-religous fissures in the social fabric, which he believes are breaking the French Republic apart. In the departure [of young Frenchmen] for Syria to engage in*

jihad and undergo martyrdom, there is the natural and concrete sequel of their virtual indoctrination..."

Clausen explains how Kepel sees the polarized French domestic political scene as the reason for the loss of identity in traditional national values: "*Kepel argues that France is particularly susceptible to online jihadist propaganda because of a breakdown of allegiance to the once-fundamental French principles of secularism and color-blindness. On the political left and right alike, a defection from core French republican virtues has created 'ruptures' within the nation and given rise to a new form of identity politics. On the left, multiculturalism and an insistence on respect for difference are usurping laïcité, the traditional French republican ideal of civic secularism. (Anti-Semitism, long present on the French right, now taints the left as well.) On the right, xenophobia and ultranationalism have pushed voters into the arms of the populist, anti-immigrant National Front.*"

With regard to the lack of economic opportunities for the unemployed or underemployed Muslim youth, Clausen explains that Kepel "*...does not argue that economic stagnation or the inability to integrate immigrants has driven terrorist recruitment. Instead, he blames dangerous forms of Islam. He points to the emergence of ultraconservative Salafi enclaves, which have bred a new generation of violent Islamists. Salafi preachers advocate a whole-life version of Islam that isolates Muslim communities and encourages confrontation with the infidel French state, which Salafists regard with 'suspicion, fear, or indifference...' And lax government supervision of mosques has allowed non-Francophonic imams to preach on the evils of French society.*"

The Danish professor then mentions another French political scientist, Olivier Roy, who authored an essay titled "Jihadism Is a Generational and Nihilistic Revolt" for *Le Monde* magazine: "*Roy argued... France's problem with angry young Muslims had nothing to do with Salafi fundamentalism... The new generation of extremists wasn't genuinely interested in religion; its members knew hardly anything about Islam.... France was dealing not with the radicalization of Islam but with the Islamization of radicalism. Groups of young men from poor urban communities were turning to Islamist extremism in a nihilistic rejection of society. In the process, they were abandoning their parents and the wider Muslim community. 'They have no place in the Muslim societies that they claim to defend.'"* French jihadists do not usually come from Salafi homes.

Despite the end of the physical Caliphate, European governments are still very worried about the effects of modern propaganda on their youth.

In January 2020, to counteract jihadist propaganda aimed at Swedish youth, *Sverige Television*, the Swedish national public television broadcaster, funded by a public service tax on personal income set by the Swedish national parliament, the *Riksdag*, aired the miniseries *Kalifat,* a police thriller that brings home the reality of deceptive indoctrination tactics. Swedish youngsters were promised extra-luxury lodgings and lifestyle within the surrounding of an idealist community in the service of Allah. These young men and women would then travel to Raqqa in Syria via Turkey, expecting to live their pious lives in mansions as depicted in images that had been stolen from glitzy Dubai real estate websites.

The same mendacious recruiting methods were used across Europe, and history is, unfortunately, full of the use of deceptive propaganda to enlist naïve cannon fodder. So is the continuous existence of the utopian reality as a motivator to fight and realize a new dream where everyone, especially disenfranchised youth, has a vital protagonist part to play.

Whether for jihadist dreams or criminal organizations, disaffected youth can rely on glossy propaganda videos and well-packaged conspiracy theories, TV series like *Gomorra*, about the *Camorra*, the Neapolitan mafia, or *Narcos*, a series about Mexico's narco-trafficking cartels, as a source of identification and inspiration.

In today's media-driven world, the spread and effectiveness of deceiving recruiting tools is extremely concerning because it leverages a far-stronger factor in the pull to join such groups and be willing to be slaughtered on their behalf—the human desire to belong.

In 2012, *William B. Swann Jr.* and *Michael D. Buhrmester* wrote a paper for the Association for Psychological Science titled "Identity Fusion." The premise of their study is that: *"Identity fusion is a visceral sense of oneness with a group and its individual members that motivates personally costly, pro-group behaviors. Past approaches, most notably social-identity theory, have assumed that, when people align with groups, the group category eclipses both the personal self and the relationships among individual group members. Also, social-identity researchers have focused on intergroup processes. In contrast, fusion theory emphasizes the role of the personal self and intragroup relationships in extreme pro-group action. Strongly fused persons are especially inclined to endorse pro-group action when either the personal or the social self is salient, when physiological arousal is high, or when they perceive that group members share essential qualities (e.g., genes, core values) with one another. Moreover, feelings of personal agency, perceptions of family-like ties to other group members, and a sense of group-related invulnerability mediate the link between identity fusion and pro-group behaviors."*

Muslim youth from all over the world joined The Caliphate in droves because they did not feel they belonged in their nations. They did not feel represented, as traditional identifiers like nationality, family, and ethnicity were competing at best and contradictory at worst. They joined because they felt that the opportunity to self-actualize lay elsewhere.

In February 2019, the Belgian *Royal Higher Institute for Defence* circulated a study by Prof. *Elena Aoun* of the Université Catholique de Louvain and Dr. *Didier Leroy* of Belgium's Center for Security and Defence Studies. The study, which was titled *"Crossed Views on Jihadism: The Engagement of Middle Eastern Fighters in Syria,"* aptly focused on the phenomenon of the mobilization of identities across borders.

Belgium's Muslim youth have been plagued by the same deceptive recruiting attempts that have preyed on their French, Dutch, British, and Scandinavian co-religionists.

When I started looking at Belgium, I had initially believed that psychological, economic, and alphabetization were the primary factors, rather than religious ideology, behind these youths' gullibility, because I had seen non-Muslim women and men joining the Islamist cause. I then had to analyze Belgium's domestic radicalization as part of the much-publicized judicial fights over the repatriation of two Belgian women and their children who had gone to join The Caliphate and were interned in a Syrian refugee camp.

The case that I had the opportunity to review created the precedent for more Belgian nationals like *Nadia Baghouri, Adel Mezroui, Jessie Van Eetvelde,* and *Sabah Hammani* to seek Belgian government assistance in their desire to be repatriated. Also, these women had traveled to Syria to become "Caliphate brides." They had then traveled back to Belgium to give birth to their children, hence ensuring they would benefit from Belgian citizenship and a very decent, publicly funded health service. They had then traveled with their children back to Syria to finally end up in a refugee camp. I am now guessing that their original home, which they had left because they felt it did not provide for their happiness, or even a Belgian jail, must have looked like paradise in comparison to a Syrian refugee camp.

These four mothers took the Belgian government to court, claiming a right to evacuation back to Belgium, and won. However, this time, as opposed to the two Belgian mothers in the case that I analyzed, they were not included in the court's order, making it the first ruling to be issued solely for children.

Belgium's military and its security services have, therefore, been very sensitive to the issue of identity mobilization, across borders, in the name of the jihadist dream.

The study by Aoun and Leroy was based on more than 50 "semi-directive" interviews conducted in Lebanon with a variety of parties across the political and religious spectrum.

Its findings revealed that:

"...*On one side, Hezbollah's (Shia) operatives are bound to a powerful top-down organization with an agenda underpinned by geostrategic calculations and identity politics; for this group, asabiyya ('esprit de corps') has proven to be paramount. On the other side, the involvement of Sunnis takes place on an individual basis within networks of jihadis built almost exclusively on the activation of religious identities and enmities; for these mostly atomized actors, social anomie (i.e., the loss of social bearings) has been found essential. Interestingly, the research has shown that both of these obviously opposite social experiences (excess and lack of belonging) converge in making identity so prone to activation that individuals opt for a path leading to a likely if not a certain death in a cross-border conflict that is not theirs at first sight.... These dynamics [relate] to broader factors, and notably to the failure of the Lebanese state and society to build a cohesive national project. Both these factors have led to excessive polarization and ensuing narratives of victimization, hence sustaining the cultivation of transnational primary identities at the expense of national belonging.*"

In my personal estimate, during the fight to eliminate the physical Caliphate, we have killed in excess of 150,000 Iraqi, Syrian, and other foreign fighters and civilians.

Although this is a very difficult reality for me to accept, as I have religiously mandated respect for the sanctity of human life, I cannot shake off my belief that, in order to physically eliminate The Caliphate, the bloodshed was lamentable yet necessary.

I do feel deep sorrow for all these young men and women who were duped into giving up their lives or who felt that death was a much-better alternative to the life they had. Killing The Caliphate might have meant small numbers in comparison to the millions who perished during World War II's failed utopias, but the number is still too significant for all of us not to pause and seek long-lasting solutions to stop spilling blood before it becomes necessary—to increase the space between shouting and shooting.

The King's Game

> History always looms large—ancient cultures
> fight their wars alongside the ghosts of their
> past. Once a battle has been fought, the echo of
> the fighting warriors, the cries of the dying, the
> thumps of horses' hoofs reverberate forever.

IN THE PREVIOUS CHAPTER, we remembered those who very recently gave up their lives in the name of identity in the context of this history-long chess game. But who are the main players—the primary pieces in the Greater Middle East chessboard?

Chess is a board game believed to be of Indian origin—the *chaturanga,* developed around 600 AD. Like many other products from the exotic Far East, it used the well-traveled trade routes to get into Persia and into the Islamic world. It found eager players in the Middle East, as the Persians were already playing a similar game supposedly invented by *Xerxes I,* the king who failed to conquer Greece, around 500 BC.

The game was then "transported" into Europe by the *Umayyad* Arabs through the Islamic colony of *Andalus* in Southern Spain (Hispania) in the 9th century. Like many other things coming from Arabia, the Europeans happily adopted the game. It was the Europeans that transformed the game from mere entertainment to a war game designed to develop strategic mindsets.

In Europe, the war game was codified through a number of books, first by the Portuguese *Pedro Damião,* who wrote a book in 1512 that went through eight editions, describing the rules of the game, offering advice on strategy, presenting a selection of chess problems, analyzing a few "*openings,*" and offering advice regarding "blindfold chess." In his book, the *powers* of the individual chess *pieces* were clearly defined.

Damião's book was then followed by the *Libro de la invencion liberal y arte del juego del axedrez*—the Book of the liberal invention and art of the game of chess, by the Spanish *Ruiz Lopez de Segura* and the *Das Schach—oder Königsspiel*—The King's Game, by the German *Augustus the Younger, Duke of Brunswick-Lüneburg.*

For those who are not familiar with chess, an **opening** refers to the initial moves and may also be known as "a defense." In addition to referring to specific move sequences, the opening is the first phase of a chess game, the other phases being the "middlegame" and the "endgame." The thousands of openings or defenses follow codified strategies with names such as *King's Indian Defense,* the *Sicilian* or *French Defense,* and many other tactical attributions. It is a fascinating field of study. It is both Machiavellian and Sun Tzuist. It is the ultimate "psychology of war" board game.

The Middle East is a 3.5 million-square-mile chessboard.

If, in the chess game, the pieces' powers were defined by Europeans as codified by Pedro Damião in 1512, in the modern Middle East, the pieces' current powers were also defined by Europeans, between 1918 and 1948. The **opening** that still defines today's strategies was played during that 30-year period. It should be aptly named "*The English Job,*" as the Iranians—ever distrustful of the British—call anything treacherous "*This is 'an English job'!*".

There have been entire libraries written on the subject. In the interest of brevity, I will, therefore, focus on those countries that I believe are the main players as if they were the board's eight major chess pieces.

In chess, the formation has eight minor pieces, or pawns, and eight major pieces. Pawns are considered to be the least powerful pieces on the chessboard. They are still very important in the general strategic unfolding of any scenario but very limited in what they can singularly do. Traditionally, being defined as a pawn is not flattering and can cause outrage, but that shouldn't be the case, as all players have varying degrees of importance in the strategic play of the region.

I will not dedicate any in-depth analysis to the Middle East pawns or even name them. However, they can be identified by process of exclusion. I am not discounting at all the important role that these pieces play in the region. I hold these pawns in very high consideration, for their balancing acts, which require superior diplomatic ability. As stated in my introduction, these small emirates, sultanates, and kingdoms must deal with not only security threats stemming from global actors and regional rivals but also with internal dynamics, such as ethno-sectarian rifts or social resentments. As their security and economic development remain a top priority, they are in a constant balancing act between the needs for autonomy versus security, and the fear of abandonment by a major sponsor versus loss of independence and legitimacy.

Among the eight major pieces, there are four minor pieces—two knights and two bishops. The two knights in the Middle East are China and Russia. Disruptive, nimble, and quick, yet limited in their reach and generally outmatched by the Queen. The two bishops are Turkey and Israel, both with long reach but limited, for historical and cultural reasons, effectiveness.

The remaining four major pieces are the two rooks, which are very valuable, as they are solid, have a long reach, and are an historical safe bet with regard to their ability to endure; they are Iran and Egypt. The Queen, the all-powerful, all-reaching piece, is the United States of America, while the King is the Middle East itself. It is the result of the strategic performance and interaction of all pieces. Powerful, yet fragile. If it falls, the game is over.

The British-American historian *Bernard Lewis* was a prominent Oriental history expert. In his *Digest of the Middle East*, Lewis stated: "*The Middle East is not a geographical region; rather it is a concept that is based upon Western orientation to the world.*"

The Western posture toward this region—its sequence of **openings**—is, in my opinion, defined by three historical moments (acts). The first two are linked to the rise and fall of the Roman empire. *Andrew Skitt Gilmour*, a 32-year veteran of the Central Intelligence Agency, and I share a common belief and approach to analysis and policymaking in the Middle East. We both seek for answers in the distant past. In his "*A Middle East Primed for a New Thinking—Insights and Policy Options from the Ancient World,*" Skitt Gilmour goes as far back as to ancient Greece to explain modern Middle Eastern dynamics. I start with Rome and the destruction of Jerusalem by *Titus'* legions, in 70 AD, which kick-started the global expansion of Christianity, and with the fall of Constantinople in 1453, the Byzantine capital of the Eastern Roman Empire, which sanctioned the apotheosis of Islamic expansion. The third defining act happened 463 years later; it was the Sykes-Picot partition strategy and the creation of the State of Israel.

What is behind that Western orientation to the Arab world? Arabs are not the only ones who recall events that occurred 600 years prior as if they had happened last week. Europeans do, too. Events that have shaped history 1300 years ago are still shaping today's West's perceptions, trust, alliances, and foreign policies.

Great Britain and France, two major chess pieces at the formation of the modern Middle East, are still present on the board, but they are relegated to pawns' reach. I feel that these two nations' Middle East policies have changed very little since the time of Francois Georges-Picot and Mark Sykes, but their current reach is very much reduced due to weak domestic economies and political polarization.

In his book *The English Job,* former British Foreign Minister *Jack Straw* correctly recalls the poignant joke that regularly occurs among British diplomats: *"Iran is the only country in the world which still regards the United Kingdom as a superpower."*

In the Middle East, as in the rest of the world, access is power, and both France and Great Britain have seen their accessibility in the area severely hindered by recent history and by dwindling domestic budgets.

For the past 70 years, despite some initial opposition from the now defunct Soviet bloc, the Queen—the USA—has been the sole major foreign power, operating virtually unchallenged in the Middle East region across all elements of national power.

The Queen and the Rooks
America, Iran, and Egypt

> People talk about centuries-old victories as
> if they had happened yesterday, and they all
> dream that their forefathers fought there.

S INCE THE 1950s, America, the strongest economic and military power that the world has ever seen, has become the Christian West's face in the Middle East and Islamic countries, all around the world. It is, at the same time, admired, loathed, and feared by Muslims.

A month after the 9/11 attacks, *Usama bin Laden*, the leader of *Al Qaeda*, was interviewed by *Tayseer Alouni* for Al Jazeera television. When asked by Alouni, *"Al Qaeda is facing now a country that leads the world militarily, politically, technologically. Surely, the Al Qaeda organization does not have the economic means that the United States has. How can Al Qaeda defeat America militarily?"* Bin Laden replied: *"This battle is not between Al Qaeda and the U.S. This is a battle of Muslims against the global crusaders…"*

Bruce Riedel, a former CIA officer deeply involved in the Middle East and author of the book *Beirut 1958—How America's Wars in the Middle East Began,* indicates the deployment of 14,000 U.S. military personnel during *Operation Blue Bat* in Lebanon (15 July 1958 to 25 October 1958) as the first act of American activism in the Middle East.

In the book, Riedel, who emphasizes that his book is not a history book but an essay on foreign policy, stresses how, in the aftermath of

World War II and the Korean War, *Dwight D. Eisenhower*, even if he had never been in combat, fully grasped the dire price of war. Despite understanding the risky reality of further bloodshed, Eisenhower did not hesitate to resort to the use of his Department of Defense's capacity abroad in order to alleviate hard domestic-policy realities, as he was behind in the presidential election polls.

At that time, the Soviets were being perceived as ahead in the space race, and momentous and courageous decisions had to be taken to sway the public opinion's approval. This moment might have been the first but will not be the last time that American military operations in the Middle East have been undertaken in order to address a domestic-policy climate rather than for foreign-affairs reasons.

Riedel, who both grew up in the Middle East and extensively worked across the region, believes that the USA has tended to overreact in the area, before waiting for the dust to settle. This leads to ineffective solutions.

Richard Engel, Chief Foreign Correspondent for NBC News and author of the book *And Then All Hell Broke Loose—Two Decades in the Middle East*, states that the Middle East flares suddenly. Signs of events to come can be seen in advance, but once strife starts, it is generally uncontrollable. He believes that this is the result of a cultural and emotional attitude which is common to both those *"Middle Eastern nations with long histories and no oil and those that have lots of oil and no history."*

I do not fully concur with Riedel's analysis on the American tendency to overreact. There is merit to his observation, however, I believe the quick American reaction, typically a military operation, has often been conducted for the purpose of messaging the domestic audience rather than a codified strategy in U.S. Middle Eastern policy.

Since the advent of ever-present media messaging, the American military is primarily an instrument of domestic policy—an instrument that most administrations use for foreign-policy intervention to safeguard American interests abroad, but whose ultimate benefit is approval ratings back home.

The United States has a cultural propensity to heavily rely on its military muscle as its primary instrument of national power. The military instrument, despite doctrinal subjugation to diplomacy, is still widely considered the prominent one by the American public opinion and its policymakers. When a dangerous situation flares around the world, the first reaction of the American people has often been *"Send in the Marines"* or, now, *"Send in the Navy SEALs"* rather than *"Send in the diplomats."*

When I hear about this matter from foreign nationals, both military personnel and civilians, there is always a consensus of opinion—most foreigners feel that, except for Pearl Harbor in 1941 and New York in 2001, the American public has witnessed war only through their television sets and the conditions of their returning warriors. Foreigners also feel that America has an economic need to continuously engage in armed confrontations in order to keep one of the pillars of its economy—the military-industrial complex—going. Jokes are frequently made about the American entertainment industry and the need for the nation to fight wars, so that blockbuster movies can be produced about them.

The same foreigners would then concur on the need for a strong referee that will not hesitate to use force when needed. They celebrate America's willingness to lose its soldiers to defend other people's freedom, and admit that it feels comforting to have a friend one can rely on for protection. America's defect is, in the eye of its allies, also its most precious quality.

There are many who argue that the employment of America's military muscle might be currently changing—not because of domestic policies but because of a global socio-cultural and economic shift.

The world has witnessed how U.S. military deployment in the Middle East has morphed over the past 10 years. Ten years ago, the

United States had more than 150,000 troops in Iraq; today, the force size is less than 10 percent of that number. However, the firepower and technological superiority that those 15,000 personnel enjoy is still a guarantee that, when America speaks, the Middle East continues to listen.

Across the world, there might now be a consensus that, after 19 years of an ineffective and incredibly expensive Global War on Terrorism, war can no longer be justified as an alternative to diplomacy and soft power—that war is justified only in self-defense.

As I explained earlier, I believe that the term "Global War on Terrorism" might be misunderstood by many—it is a brand and not a campaign or a strategy. Today's warfare is more about counter-insurgency-enforcement operations than full-blown conflagrations between opposing armies. War, as we knew it, might no longer be a viable alternative to diplomacy, but it is, in my opinion, very much needed as a rapid-enforcement tool.

The American debate about using military versus soft power is as old as the nation's origin. America has grappled with this conundrum since its birth.

When, in the early 1860s, Union General *James Henry Carleton* marched against *Apache* and *Navajo* warriors in America's Southwest, he gave instructions to Colonel *Kit Carson* to tell the Navajo leadership: "*…This war shall be pursued against you if it takes years, now that we have begun, until you cease to exist or move. There can be no other talk on the subject.*"

Colonel Carson dutifully complied and, after defeating the Navajo nation, wrote to his superiors: "*I believe this will be the last Navajo war… I beg respectfully to call the serious attention of the government to the destitute conditions of the captives and beg for authority to provide clothing for the women and children. Every preparation will be made to plant large crops for their subsistence… Whether the Indian Department will do anything for these Indians or not you will know. But whatever is to be done should be done at once. At all events, as I wrote before to you,* **we can feed them cheaper than we can fight them.**"

John C. Cremony of the southwestern border's Boundary Commission, wrote of those wars: "*Our Government has expended millions of dollars, in driblets, since the acquisition of California, in order to reduce the Apaches and Navajos, who occupy that extensive belt of country which forms the highway for overland migration from East to the West; but we are as far from success to-day as we were twenty years ago. The reason is obvious. We have never striven to make us intelligently acquainted with those tribes. Nearly all that relates to them is quite as uncertain and indefinite to our comprehension as that which obtains in the center of Africa. Those who were the best informed on the matter, and have given it the closest attention, were, at the same time—most unfortunately—the least capable of imparting their information; while those who were almost ignorant of the subject have been the most forward to give the results of their fragmentary gleanings.*"

In foreign affairs, diplomacy's soft power, which I believe should be the primary instrument of national power, right before economic development and trade, might still not be as effective, by itself, in the Middle East.

If it is true that policy suggestions by the U.S. Department of State are too often overlooked or plainly ignored, again for domestic-policy reasons, it is also true that the Middle East chessboard has consistently been the hotbed of military operations well before America's involvement in the area.

Also, if it is true that the nature of the U.S. political system, where campaigning for political re-election every four years might not allow for long-term policy consistency, it is also true that every single superpower that has operated in the Middle East as a kingmaker has had to go to war very often—Egypt, Persia, Rome, Islam, Christianity.

The debate on the use of hard or soft powers, whether in foreign affairs or the business world, was encapsulated in an exchange I had in 1996 with *Ken Bates*, the Chairman of Chelsea Football Club, in London. He was complaining about the need for long and minutiae-focused meetings and extended negotiations. He reminded us that the Romans did not build a great empire by organizing meetings; they did it by killing anybody that got in their way.

Although I agreed with Bates' historical reference, I answered that perhaps the Roman empire had not survived because becoming too good at killing people does not master the ability to live in peace. The downside of being very good at waging war might be the inability to be good peacemakers.

I wonder how Bates would have related to the *Muawiyah Strand*, one of the basic tenets of Arab diplomacy. It is the art of relentless engagement for engagement's sake—an uninterrupted, apparently meaningless, connection between parties which occurs over the course of centuries. A process which, even if it is fruitless, provides a thin strand of connection (the Muawiyah Strand) on which something important can be built when the time is ripe.

Understanding the *"Strand of Hair Approach"* is vital for anyone who wishes to engage diplomatically in the Middle East. The source is in one of the holy Islamic Hadiths:

"The Messenger of Allah (sal Allahu alaihi wa sallam) said: The best of affairs is that which is far from both extremes. [Al-Bayhaqi] Muawiyah was once asked, How did you manage to be a governor for twenty years and then a Caliph for twenty years?" He replied, "I placed a strand of hair between myself and the people. I would hold it from one end, and they would hold it from the other. If they pulled it from their end, I would loosen it from mine so that the strand of hair would not break. If they loosened it from their end, I would pull on it from mine. If both partners in a couple are stubborn, then they cannot live together in happiness. Similarly, two stubborn people can never be friends for long. A fire is not put out by fire; it will only increase the flames. Similarly, coldness cannot be removed with coldness. So, don't deal with a stubborn person by using stubbornness; it will only result in fireworks. Remember

*Muawiyah's Strand of Hair approach to deal effectively with people.
Keep your behavior moderate and flexible while, at all times, within the
bounds of Sharia."*

For countries expecting quick, tangible results from foreign
engagement, the Muawiyah Strand would be a maddening endeavor.
Therefore, the immense gap between the Islamic foreign-policy style
and the short-term focus of American audiences does not produce
consistent, long-term policies in the region.

American diplomats have often spoken about this gap and
have appropriately counseled political administrations, only to see
their arguments set aside, as presidents crafted policies to please
their domestic audiences. *Thomas Pickering,* former U.S. Ambassador
to Jordan, Israel, and the U.N., once stated:

*"One definition of insanity is doing the same thing over and over
again, getting the same results over and over again, yet expecting a different result every time from the one you got last time. If you accept that
as a working definition of insanity, then the U.S. policy toward Iran has
been certifiably insane for nearly three decades."*

Despite the structural electoral impediment to crafting consistent,
long-term foreign policies, the USA can rely on the military constant.
Most U.S. administrations, whether Republican or Democrat, have
a more pragmatic, business-like approach to both national security
and the use of Department of Defense capacity.

In the USA, the Department of Defense (DoD), is the agency
of national choice. It is ultimately Congress and the American people
who do not wish this agency's capacity and reach to diminish. They
have come to rely on it for their safety needs, whether that implies
revenue and employment in their home states, natural disasters, the
threat of terrorism, or pandemic events.

DoD might be the largest corporation in the world. Although
some argue that it is run like the largest welfare program in the nation,
it still provides a capacity that can hardly be offered elsewhere. DoD
might not be efficient, but it is extremely effective. DoD is extremely

effective at, among many things, waging war. It is famously not effective at peacemaking and nation-building, but that is not what DoD was built for. As one of my former economics professors used to teach: If you have purchased a tiger, you had better put it to work in a circus and keep it busy. If you cannot find a circus, you had better build one. Because even when you do not use the tiger for work, it sure keeps eating.

The American military-industrial complex model is very well understood in the Middle East, and both rooks—Egypt and Iran—use their own versions, with the same economic models, and the same focus to domestic audiences.

With regard to the significance of America's military-industrial complex, when I teach Comparative National Security Analysis, I encourage my students, who are mostly military professionals, to read *How Everything Became War and the Military Became Everything: Tales from the Pentagon,* by *Rosa Brooks.*

Ms. Brooks, a former DoD senior executive, who is married to a military officer, affirms that the reality of DoD being the American people's agency of choice is not lost on other government agencies that see their own role infringed upon by the continuous need to expand DoD's area of expertise.

Relationships between military and civilian personnel in the inter-agency world are pretty good, but at the national strategic level, the resentment that the military has generated by expanding its role, assuming responsibility for all manner of unlikely projects, is very palpable. In its efforts to stem the growth of future generations of terrorists, the Pentagon not only resorts to its kinetic capacity but also sponsors peace concerts in Africa, trains militias in international humanitarian law, distributes soccer balls with anti-extremist slogans in Iraq, builds wells and solar-power facilities in rural mountain villages, trains judges in Afghanistan, sends doctors and hospital ships to stem pandemic outbreaks, enforces against narcotics trafficking, and builds national border walls—anything to promote stability both domestically and in volatile nations. Recently, it has even been asked to field its forces to guard against American protesters and looters in the nation's capital.

Most of these initiatives abroad drive State Department personnel and aid workers—the people who would ordinarily be charged with such efforts—absolutely insane. Some of these initiatives at home drive enforcement agencies, politicians, and former military leaders absolutely insane.

Today, U.S. military personnel do not just "*kick doors, kill people, and break stuff.*" Instead, they analyze computer codes, inoculate children, rescue people from floods, build Ebola isolation wards, eavesdrop on electronic communications, advise on Hollywood blockbusters, develop soap operas, patrol for pirates, interdict drug smugglers, evacuate populations affected by humanitarian disasters, try terrorists, build refugee camps, and patrol borders to stem immigration.

As mentioned, in the past, when America felt it had a security issue around the world, the typical response would be "*to send in the Marines.*" In today's age, it doesn't even have to be a security issue—anything that necessitates quick solutions, short-term efficacy, reliable logistics, and impeccable security protection, anything at all, you name it, DoD provides it all. DoD has become the nation's ultimate Walmart.

In both Egypt and Iran, the military tentacular dominance of the national economies is absolute. They both are military and police states. This model makes them both formidable partners or adversaries.

In Egypt, the model is seven decades old but has steadily accelerated under the rule of presidents *Hosni Mubarak* and *Abdel Fattah el-Sisi,* himself a military officer. The Egyptian military controls 20 percent of public spending, and it is not subject to external audit or parliamentary oversight. It owns land from which it receives rental income, and it manufactures, imports, and distributes pharmaceutical products and food items, as those are considered strategic staples. It is exempt from taxes and income duties. The Egyptians have taken a page out of the American military-industrial complex manual. The Persians have, too.

In a May 2015 article titled "Who Really Controls Iran's Economy?" by *Emanuele Ottolenghi* and *Saeed Ghasseminejad* for *National Interest* magazine, the two experts from the Foundation for Defense of Democracies and at its Center on Sanctions and Illicit Finance, state:

"While it is true that in 2005, the Supreme Leader launched a large privatization drive, mandating the government to sell most state-owned industries, the program did not exactly empower the country's fledgling private sector. Its main beneficiaries were foundations controlled by the Islamic Republic's deep state, including the military, especially the Revolutionary Guards and Khamenei. One can speculate about how dominant the economic position of these entities in the Iranian economy is. But there is no question that the IRGC, owing to this 'privatization,' has gained significant influence over Iran's economy and its political system... (the strategic staples industry) is firmly in the hands of the business empires of the Supreme Leader's and Iran's military foundations, which are overwhelmingly in the hands of the revolutionary guards... We have been tracking the intervention of military foundations—both the Guard Corps' and the armed forces'—into Iran's stock market (the Tehran Stock Exchange) since 2011. Military-controlled companies are mostly concentrated in strategic sectors such as oil, mining, telecommunications, petrochemicals, automotive, banking, and construction. As of April, the portfolio of military foundations consisted of 26 publicly traded firms with a market value of $17.5 billion—almost 20 percent of Tehran's Stock Exchange market value. The Supreme Leader's business empire accounts for an estimated additional 5 percent through three foundations he controls: Setad Ejraiye, the Foundation of the Oppressed and Disabled (or Mostazafan Foundation), and Rey Group. We estimate that together, they control one fourth of the stock exchange." The two authors supported these statements with in-depth research and concluded: *"Finally, the Guard Corps and other military and paramilitary forces have a high share*

of Iran's underground economy, estimated at somewhere between 6 and 36 percent of Iran's GDP, which includes commissions from smuggling operations and reportedly a hand in the drug traffic that crosses Iran on its way to Europe from Afghanistan. Putting a price tag on such activities is difficult. Relying on their stock-exchange ownership is an adequate, though obviously incomplete, indicator of their financial clout. But to claim that the privatization drive has created a more complex picture of corporate ownership is to miss the forest for the trees."

Even if the similarity between the military-industrial complexes of the USA, Egypt, and Iran might be overstated, especially because America does not have the soft-power craftiness that the Egyptians and the Persians have had to develop and rely on in the course of the past 5,000 years, this is the reality by which Egypt and Iran are, after the USA, the most powerful pieces in the Middle East.

Without the direct support of the strongest piece on the board, the Queen, not even nuclear-armed Israel, or wealthy Saudi Arabia could withstand a prolonged full-frontal military confrontation with either of these two rooks.

If, for the first time in recent Arab history, one of these two nations ever decided that another all-out war is necessary because their very existence is at stake, no Middle Eastern country could take the full brunt of their military might. Even if bloody, the minor wars that Israel had to fight against its Arab neighbors so far pale in comparison to the sheer determinate brutality of a war like the Iran-Iraq war, which lasted eight years because both countries believed that their national survival was at stake. Statistics regarding that war's death toll vary, but it is estimated that Iran lost up to one million souls and Iraq half of that. In today's age, Egypt and Iran are still the only two nations in the Middle East whose regimes can afford to lose that number of people and come out stronger from it.

"There are only two nations in the Middle East—Egypt and Iran— the rest are tribes with flags." The phrase was related to me by *Karim Sadjapour* in Washington, DC. Karim is a Senior Fellow at the

Carnegie Institute for International Peace and one of the foremost experts on Iran. He attributed the statement to *Tahseen Bashir,* an Egyptian diplomat and historian who died in 2002.

Boutros Boutros-Ghali, the former Egyptian foreign minister and Secretary General of the United Nations, recalled a 1970s exchange with his boss, *Anwar al-Sadat,* that frames how the Egyptian president viewed the Gulf Arab states: *"... the semi-countries in the gulf... which are but a little band of no political or true economic value."*

Egypt and Iran carry the weight, the cohesion, and the intact cultural heritage of millennia. Thousands of years of resilience—successes and failures, booms and busts, glorious victories, and tragic losses. Egyptians and Persians share a belief—that their nations were built by God to endure, unlike the rest of the Middle East, which is merely a Western creation from the ashes of the Ottoman Empire. This Western creation is barely a century old, and, because it is man-made, it must be forcefully kept together by its creators.

Perhaps the best way to describe the Iranian cultural and national cohesiveness was offered by *Uri Lubrani* in an interview with *Trita Parsi,* the Iranian-born co-founder and Executive Vice president of the Quincy Institute for Responsible Statecraft. Parsi is also the founder and former president of the National Iranian American Council.

Uri Lubrani might be the best testimonial to describe the strength of Persian cultural character because he was a legendary Israeli diplomat. He joined the *Haganah* in 1944 and served in the *Palmach.* He assisted the *Aliyah Bet* operations to smuggle illegal Jewish immigrants into Palestine and, in 1946, was sent to France to command a training camp for English-speaking Jewish volunteers whom he then joined to fight in the Israeli War of Independence.

After the war ended, Lubrani served in the Middle East Department of the Israeli Foreign Ministry, to then be appointed

Deputy Adviser on Arab Affairs for Prime Minister *David Ben-Gurion*. In this role, he was dedicated to development in Arab villages and recruiting *Druze* into military service.

In 1964, he joined the diplomatic corps of the Foreign Ministry and was appointed to a number of ambassadorships, including, from 1973 to 1978, the head of the Israeli diplomatic mission in Iran.

Lubrani, who just before his death in 2018 had called for the overthrow of the Iranian regime to stop their nuclear program, was for many years the recognized go-to man between Iran and Israel—the living embodiment of an historical relationship that, despite the ever-present belligerent media propaganda for the consumption of the unknowing public, has been strongly in place since the creation of the State of Israel.

In the interview, Lubrani recounted: *"During my first visit to Iran, I visited a small village. It was a poor village; they didn't have running water and other basic facilities. But in the evening, the villagers gathered to hear one of their elders recite the Shahname. The scene of these poor villagers listening to this man reciting the Shahname by heart had a vast impact on me. Iran wasn't rich, it wasn't developed, but it was a civilization."*

The Book of Kings, or *Shahname,* is a very long epic poem written by the Persian poet *Ferdowsi* between 977 and 1010 AD and is the national epic of Greater Iran. It is a monument to Persian cohesion, as it recounts the mythical past of the Persian Empire from the creation of the world until the Arab conquest of Iran in the 7th century.

The poem, which is of central importance in Persian culture and Persian language, describes both the ethno-national cultural identity of Iran and its staunch resistance to the invaders' futile attempts to *Arabize* Persia.

Parsi, Lubrani's interviewer, authored several books on Iranian affairs and U.S. policies toward Iran. In his work *Treacherous Alliance—The Secret Dealings of Israel, Iran, and the U.S.,* he goes on to meticulously describe not only the dealings between Iran, Israel, and the U.S. but also the undeniable cultural and character similarities between the Iranians and the Israelis.

One of the most vivid descriptions is the ever-present sound of Farsi music played by Iranian-Jewish shopkeepers around Jerusalem's downtown bus terminal. The same Israelis who are still proud of their Iranian roots and, by decrying the lack of serious economic opportunities in the Promised Land, can't help dreaming of the lifestyle they left in Iran, a country which houses the second-largest Jewish population in the Middle East, outside Israel.

I have truly loved all the Middle Eastern countries that I visited. Unfortunately, I have never visited Iran. Egypt left me mesmerized. The country is coping with the typical problems associated with uncontrolled population growth. The gap between the wealthy and the poor is startling, but its people are caring and welcoming; their resilience and proud cohesion is visible everywhere one goes. In Egypt, I felt the Mediterranean legacy of my Neapolitan childhood.

Noisy, congested, and dirty Cairo could intimidate any tourist, but, with the exception of the few times when I thought that I had to protect my unaccustomed wife from potentially distressing situations, I found myself comforted by the sheer humanity of the Egyptian capital. Cairo, just like Napoli, *e' decadente e superba nei suoi riccioli di pietra*—Naples is decayed, yet superb in its stones, which resemble the curly hair of a *street urchin*. Cairo evokes the same image, as its spirited street kids reminded me of the Neapolitan street kids.

The welcoming ritual of bartering with the *souk's* shopkeepers was all too familiar for me. I felt like a medieval traveler who had crossed the Mediterranean to find, in my very uncertain Arabic, a *hanfia nafura mizrab*—an arabesque, ornate waterspout for my Roman marble fountain. I felt at home.

From Aswan to Luxor and again north to Cairo, it was an unforgettable journey back in history. A traveler cannot fail to be amazed by the depth of the historical heritage that the Egyptians can fall back on whenever they need to. Six thousand years worth of stories literally immortalized in tombs, architecture, and rituals. All of Egypt's history coming alive again in a sunset, in scents, in the sparkling reflection of the Nile.

A reason of a different nature is also behind Egypt's prominent importance in the Middle East—its enduring internal struggle with a domestic political invention that has become a global export. Anywhere you go in Egypt, the "elephant in the room" is omnipresent. It is a radical Sunni movement—*The Muslim Brotherhood (the Brotherhood)*. Why can't the Brotherhood be ignored, and why is it so important in Middle Eastern dynamics?

Because this radical movement has shaped modern history as it became the legitimate alternative and successor to *Abdel Nasser's* secular Pan-Arabic dream—its secularism seen as the project's Achille's Heel. Nasser's great project had failed, in the belief of a great number of *Muslim Brothers*, because it had ignored God's guidance in favor of the polluting compromises of *realpolitik*.

Regarded as an existential threat in Egypt and the Gulf monarchies, the Brotherhood is at the core of the *Gulf Cooperation Council* (GCC) rift and is one of the factors that are shaping current Middle Eastern alliances. Also, many legal organizations, movements, parties, and associations take inspiration from the Brotherhood and share its vision of political Islam. There is no consensus over whether the Brotherhood is a terrorist organization, especially since it officially renounces violence and fiercely opposes terrorist groups such as Al-Qaeda and Daesh. It is, however, shaping regional dynamics.

The Brotherhood is an original Egyptian export—a transnational Sunni Islamist movement with branches throughout the world. It operates under a variety of names and with multiple social and political agendas. All Brotherhood branches share a firm commitment to a rooted Islamist ideology—to restore The Caliphate and enforce the Sharia law.

In secular Egypt, armed jihad remains an integral part of the Brotherhood's ideology, as its founding bylaws explicitly state: "*The Islamic nation must be fully prepared to fight the tyrants and the enemies of Allah as a prelude to establishing an Islamic state.*"

Hassan al-Banna founded the Brotherhood in Egypt in March 1928. He firmly opposed Western secularism and laid the foundations for the movement's political activism. He saw no real difference between religion and politics. He deemed that, through jihad and aggressive political commitment, the organization should seek enhanced political power to restore The Caliphate. Once established, The Caliphate could then enforce its understanding of Islam as a theocracy through Sharia law.

Hassan al-Banna also introduced the idea that one should love death and crave a martyr's end. This ideology is best reflected in the slogan of *Hamas'* military wing, the *Al-Qassam Brigades, "We love death more than you love life."*

According to al-Banna's successor and key influential theorist of the Brotherhood, *Sayyid Qutb*, governments not based on Sharia are apostate and therefore legitimate targets of jihad.

Hassan al-Banna and Sayyid Qutb both wrote extensively on the importance of jihad. They highlighted that the greater jihad is not the internal one (against one's own demons) but rather the fight against the people and the lands of the non-believers (infidels). Thus, most extremist leaders often refer to Sayyid Qutb's book *Milestones* as one of the most important and founding texts of modern political Islam and jihadist movements.

Therefore, one can argue that the Brotherhood has provided the intellectual and theological foundation to many militant Sunni and Salafist Islamist groups.

The differences between the Brotherhood, Daesh (The Caliphate), Al-Qaeda, and other jihadist movements are mainly tactical (ways and means) rather than ideological (ends). All share the same ultimate objective of an Islamic Caliphate governed in accordance with the Sharia law, but they disagree about the methodology for implementing it. For example, many jihadist organizations and Salafists suggest that the Brotherhood is not Islamic enough and oppose the movement's concept of gradual change. From their perspective, a gradual-change strategy offers too many unnecessary concessions. However, many extremists within the Brotherhood are frustrated with its gradual-change strategy and are leaving the organization for more-militant organizations such as Al-Qaeda or Daesh. Ironically, disaffected members of the Brotherhood have joined the two terrorist organizations that the movement has consistently denounced. In this respect, *Ayman al-Zawahiri*, the Egyptian leader of Al Qaeda, after the death of Usama Bin Laden, severely criticized the Brotherhood leaders' rejection of violence and participation in politics in his book *The Bitter Harvest.*

Though the Brotherhood officially renounced violence decades ago, in 1971, some of its offshoots employ violence to achieve their ends. The Western-created Gulf monarchies have long worried about their enduring stability. These concerns have grown since late 2010, when popular uprisings started overthrowing authoritarian regimes across the Middle East and North Africa. On several occasions, the authoritarian regimes brought the political wing of the Brotherhood to power.

The political success of the Brotherhood in Tunisia (*Ennahda*) and Mohammed Morsi's election in Egypt heightened the worries of Gulf monarchies such as the Kingdom of Saudi Arabia and the United Arab Emirates, prompting reactionary tendencies that culminated with the Egyptian Army's removal of Mohammed Morsi. The acuteness of the threat was highlighted in the aftermath of Morsi's death on 17 June 2019 through the 4 August 2019 terrorist attack outside the National Cancer Institute in Cairo.

In the Sicilian Mafia, there is a tradition of evaluating allegiances and standing by analyzing the attendance at a deceased boss's funeral. The Federal Bureau of Investigation would monitor Mafia weddings and funerals for that reason. It was interesting, therefore, to see the attendance at Morsi's funeral, the first burial of an Egyptian president in a public cemetery. Although it was largely ignored in the region, and beyond the U.N.'s calls for "transparent investigations," a few leaders expressed condolences. President Erdoğan of Turkey condemned *"Egypt's tyrants"* and called for national prayer for *"brother Morsi."* Echoing the support, Iran, Tunisia's Ennahda Party, and the Jordanian branch of the Brotherhood, all mourned Morsi's death. Qatar's Sheikh *Tamim al Thani* also offered his *"deepest condolences to his family and the Egyptian people."*

Following Army General Fattah Al-Sisi's election in Egypt, Qatar welcomed some fleeing Brotherhood leaders, and Al Jazeera offered them airtime to promote their cause. These actions angered Egypt and many of the Gulf Cooperation Council (GCC) states and led them to withdraw their ambassadors, in 2014. Despite a rather quick resolution to the rift, the wound was opened and remains open. Potential for healing is limited, since Qatar continues to host leaders of Hamas, regarded as the Palestinian branch of the Brotherhood.

In June 2017, the Kingdom of Saudi Arabia, the United Arab Emirates, Bahrain, and Egypt demanded Qatar comply with a list of 13 far-reaching requirements. These requirements covered a range of long-standing policy disagreements. However, many requirements addressed concerns about Qatar's relationship with—and support to—the Muslim Brotherhood, which is indicated as an existential threat by many Arab and Gulf countries.

Though Qatar initially sided with the GCC's effort to quell the uprising in Bahrain, it subsequently became complacent to the political rise of the Brotherhood. Qatar did not consider the Sunni movement an internal threat since Doha had already dissolved its internal chapter in 1999. Qatar has rather viewed the Brotherhood as merely a new political wave, a perception which stands firm beyond the personal relationship between Qatari Sheikh *Tamim al Thani* and Egyptian-born cleric *Yussuf al-Qaradawi.*

In Turkey, no political party officially represents the Brotherhood, but some members of the leading *Justice and Development Party (AKP)*, including Turkish President Recep Erdoğan, have provided various forms of support to the Sunni movement, such as granting asylum to wanted Egyptian Muslim Brothers. These types of indirect support to the Brotherhood logically reinforced the Qatari and Turkish relationship when the GCC crisis began.

Certainly, Egypt, Bahrain, Saudi Arabia, and the United Arab Emirates have a very different perspective, viewing the rise of the Brotherhood as a major threat to their internal stability. Since the Brotherhood's long-term intent is also to establish a Caliphate, its objectives translate into the de facto toppling of Gulf monarchies.

In the following three chapters, I will attempt to describe the roles played by a nascent Ottoman Turkey, Israel's political reality, and *"Great Power"* competitors like Russia and China, in the Middle East. I might have dedicated more space to Egypt than Iran in this chapter, as the omnipresent Iran will be touched on in almost every chapter of this book, especially in the next one, which is about Iran's quasi-ally, the bishop Turkey.

However, the general statement I would like to make for effect is that, **in Middle Eastern culture, enemies are as important, if not more important, than friends.**

Israel needs Iran as much as Egypt needs the Muslim Brotherhood. Israeli military strength and nationalistic identity is not only predicated on the Zionist dream of the Jewish homeland, but they are also predicated on Iran's existence. Iran's anti-Israeli militancy and propaganda legitimize the Islamic Republic in the eyes of Muslims worldwide and guarantees continued American support for Israel. It is all interrelated and part of the big chess game. Every single piece is linked to each other.

In the same manner, Egypt's continued militarization and secularism is predicated on the existence of the Muslim Brotherhood, while the Brotherhood keeps attracting radical Sunni support and money because it is seen as a pure and pious political Islam movement ruthlessly harassed by secular *takfirs*.

The Ottoman Bishop
Turkey

"Mamma li Turchi!"

"The Turks were a real threat to everyone living on Italy's coast for centuries.

As such, they are the default for any association with barbaric, dangerous, dirty, blasphemous, etc. Kind of like now every despised and/or feared stranger is a 'Marocchino,' as Moroccan troops under the French flag were responsible for atrocities during the occupation following World War II."

Francesco Dondi
27 December 2016

UNTIL VERY RECENTLY, I would have indicated the two bishops in the Middle East to be Israel and Saudi Arabia. Recent American policies were favoring a gradual retrenchment, while empowering both Israel and Saudi Arabia to be the de facto proxies of American interests. This is a combination which might have worked well in a much simpler reality. There is nothing simple in the Middle East.

A combination of recent factors changed the board. First, a renewed U.S. fixation on dealing with Iran head-on and bringing the rivalry to the edge of military confrontation, which has resulted in an increase rather than a decrease in U.S. involvement. Second and most important, the Saudi's military setbacks, from inefficient campaigning in Yemen to inability to secure its own domestic installations, which showed to the world that Iran would take them out in a heartbeat, were it not for American military protection. Third, Saudi Arabia's political blunders, like the Khashoggi murder and Mohammad Bin Salman's questionable methods, are making the Kingdom an uncomfortable acquaintance for everyone, including the Queen—one of those distant family members whom you are embarrassed to invite to weddings. Fourth, the U.S. political decision to withdraw from Syria has provided Turkey with incredible leverage and freedom of maneuver, advantages which President Erdoğan intends to capitalize on. Although Syria might prove to be too bitter of a bite for Moscow and Ankara to chew, in the long term, it is undoubtedly a victory, for now.

For these reasons, in my opinion, Turkey has replaced Saudi Arabia among the major pieces on the board.

Saudi Arabia's lack of authentic military prowess came into full view with the dismal performance in the fight against Houthi rebels in Yemen and its clear inability to fend off the Iranian threat, which portrays vulnerability across the region. Military prowess is not only a function of superior equipment and weaponry; it is primarily a matter of psychological disposition. The will to fight is vital to a nation's military power, and the mighty warriors of the Saud clan may be long gone.

The Saudis' inability to fight efficiently without American support and without the labor provided by nationals of poor countries is memorialized in a 22 September 2019 feature for the British newspaper *The Guardian*, titled *"Saudi Arabia won't attack Iran. But it may pay someone else to."*

Nesrine Malik, a Sudanese-born, London-based columnist and author, states: *"There is a longstanding joke told in the Middle East about Saudi Arabia's reluctance to fight its own wars. "Saudi Arabia will fight until the last Pakistani," the punchline goes, in reference to the fact that Pakistani troops have long supported Saudi military endeavors. The punchline has expanded lately to include the Sudanese, a recent addition to the Saudi army's ground troops. Saudi Arabia is accustomed to buying labor that it deems too menial for its citizens, and it extends that philosophy to its army. There is always a poorer country ready to send cannon fodder for the right price. The military assault in Yemen is sometimes referred to as "the Arab coalition," a respectable term for a Saudi-led group of combatants that, in addition to allies in the Gulf, includes forces from Egypt, Jordan, and Morocco, as well as Sudanese child soldiers, whose deaths are handsomely compensated for with cash paid to their families back home. When asked what fighting in Yemen under the command of the Saudis had been like, some returning Sudanese troops said that Saudi military leaders, feeling themselves too precious to advance too close to the frontline, had given clumsy instructions by satellite phones to their hired troops, nudging them in the general direction of hostilities. Where things were too treacherous, Saudi and coalition air forces simply dropped bombs from high-flying planes, inflating civilian casualties. This is how Saudi fights: as remotely as possible, and paying others to die..."*

Turkey might not have the money and the military equipment of the Saudis, but it has a well-known will to fight, with or without allies—an historical attitude that the Turks have successfully demonstrated not only during the Ottoman Empire but more recently in Korea, Cyprus, Libya, and Syria. The Turkish republic is also experiencing another massive national identity shift under President Erdoğan, who is attempting to rally the base around the dream of an Ottoman resurgence. Turks believe that they deserve a place among the world's power shakers because they stand on the shoulders of Ottoman giants.

If I had to look back at history to identify a traditional rivalry which is now again affecting the modern Middle East, I would point not only to the Western Christian vs. Ottoman Islamic power struggle but also to the long legacy of inter-Islamic rivalry between Saudi Arabia and Turkey, the two major regional Sunni Muslim powers—a rivalry which dates back at least four centuries.

On 6 July 1517, the Arabian Peninsula came under Ottoman rule. In the religious realm, the *Abbasid* caliphate was abolished, and *Selim* I established the Ottoman caliphate, which lasted until 1924. To ensure its legitimacy over the holy sites of Islam, Turkey claimed the title of custodian of the two most important holy mosques—*Mecca* and *Medina*. The Ottoman Empire thus included nearly all territories where Islam was practiced and became widely regarded as Islam's religious and military leader, in the eyes of both Muslims and of Western foes.

Thus, the Ottoman Empire took the lead as the Islamic unifier, the face of militant Pan-Arabism across the world. The West did not stand still. The loss of Byzantium in 1453 was still very vivid in the West's mind, and so was the loss of Jerusalem in 1187. As in other times before, in the last minutes of the game, the West rallied back and overcame internal disputes to unify and stem the Turkish advance.

Turkey's decline started almost immediately after reaching its apex. It started on the sea rather than on land, in the Battle of Lepanto (1571), an epic battle spearheaded by Spanish and Italian naval forces. Almost invincible on land, the Ottoman Empire had, in its fleets, its weak spot. As an aspect of their cultural heritage, Muslims make great seafarers, raiders, and traders but have lacked the will to build fleets which could compete against the Western bloc in the long term. The same applies for Arab and Turkish navies of today.

It was in response to perceived Ottoman oppression that one of the most important ideologies of today's age was created by a Saudi Arab, *Mohammed ibn Abdel Wahhab*. He rallied the Bedouin tribes of the Arabian Peninsula under the banner of Wahhabism, in 1744–1745, and sought to establish the First Saudi State.

Wahhabism, its Egyptian derivate Salafism, and the Muslim Brotherhood are today's most destabilizing factors of Muslim creation in the Middle East.

In 1811, the fundamentalist Wahhabis of Arabia, led by the al-Saud family, revolted against the Ottomans, who reacted and seized the Saudi capital of *Diriya* (outskirts of Riyadh), on 11 September 1818. The whole city was destroyed, and the Turkish sultan sent *Abdullah bin Saud* to Istanbul, where he was displayed in a cage and beheaded outside the *Hagia Sophia* mosque. According to some historians, his body was even propped up in public for three days with his severed head under his arm.

It was then that the Ottoman made up their mind on the nature of the Saudis—they were bloodthirsty murderers who had looted the holy city of *Karbala* in Iraq, slaughtering 4,000 Shias and later destroying many shrines in Mecca and Medina. Today's average Turk still believes that Saudis cannot be trusted and, if it were not for their oil, they would still be herding camels and raiding weaker tribes for a living. The Turks believe that the Saud's current ruling family has treachery in their blood, since the father of King Salman, and the founder of the current Saudi state, King *Abdulaziz,* went from being a subjugated and frightened vassal of the Ottomans to fighting against the Turks during World War I to supporting their complete expulsion from Arabia. The Saudi-sponsored execution of journalist Jamal Khashoggi, on Turkish soil, was perceived by Ankara as an infringement of Turkish territorial integrity and a deliberate sign of disrespect.

On the other hand, memories in the Middle East last for millennia. The modern House of Saud, despite being a far cry from the warrior elite of its founders, can hardly forget their ancestors' fate. Neither can they forget the failure of a Second Saudi State (1824), destroyed by yet another Ottoman military intervention, in alliance with the *al-Rashid,* a rival Arabian tribe, in 1871.

At the beginning of the 20th century, the Ottoman Empire continued to control most of the Peninsula, but, starting in 1902, ibn Saud, with the support of the West, slowly recaptured control of the peninsula, with full control coming in 1918, when the Allied powers of World War I took apart the Ottoman imperial possessions in the Middle East. It was a strategic partition, one which failed to take into account the local historical mosaic and was aimed at catering to the practical needs of a West afflicted by heavy war debt and, therefore, reliant on energy resources and the need for stability.

The Ottoman retreat from the Arabian Peninsula created another enduring dynamic. In 1916, again with support from Great Britain, *Hussein bin Ali,* the *Hashemite* Sharif of Mecca, a rival of the al-Sauds, had led a pan-Arab revolt against the Ottoman Empire to create a united Arab state. The Hussein family had been convinced to fight on the side of the Allies, with the promise of a crown over a liberated Arabian Peninsula. Instead, after the fight, the Husseins were moved, by the French/British entente, to rule the newly formed kingdoms of Iraq and Jordan. The mistrust between the Hashemites and the Saudis has its origins in that realignment.

Since the creation of the Kingdom of Saudi Arabia in 1932, the Saudis have worked hard to eliminate remaining traces of their country's Ottoman past. The removal and disowning of cultural heritage was considered a treacherous act of war by the Turks, a memory which has not faded.

With that, relations between Turkey and Saudi Arabia have been mainly frosty at best and briefly conciliatory at times. In 1974, during the Turkish *Operation Attila* in Cyprus, Saudi Arabia, along with Afghanistan, Iran, Pakistan, and Libya, politically and financially supported Turkey through donations of oil and cash.

At the beginning of the '90s, to compensate for the economic losses of the first Gulf War, Saudi Arabia and the Gulf Cooperation Council (GCC) granted billions of dollars in aid to Turkey for economic support and military purchases. In 2015, Saudi Arabia agreed to support a Turkey-backed coalition of militant groups under the umbrella of *Jaish al-Fatah,* in Syria. Syria routinely agitates Turkey as well as Saudi Arabia, but Turkey has key security concerns regarding the 3.5 million Syrian refugees who fled into Turkey and the PKK-affiliated Kurds.

The relationship then headed south, in the early 2000s, with the arrival of Recep Tayyip Erdoğan and his AKP party; their ties to the Muslim Brotherhood revived the political-religious competition with the Wahhabi kingdom and began to peak in the 2010s with the onset of the Arab Spring.

Modern Turkey might no longer be the secularist dream of *Kemal Ataturk,* but it is still fiercely opposed to Wahhabism and its Egyptian derivate *Salafism,* and it has used the full might of its security services to fight both ideologies. The Turks have deep distrust for the Saudis' economic support of Salafist movements, and such distrust increased further when the Kingdom's anti-Iranian support for the Syrian Kurds was revealed.

Turkish president Erdoğan proclaimed that Turkey *"is the only country that can lead the Muslim world,"* and he has a long, history-backed claim behind such a statement. He has been steadily working to increase influence in the Middle East, both with diplomacy and with military alliances, to overcome his country's two most important limitations—geopolitical restrictions and language.

On the geopolitical side, he has ousted Saudi proxies from Somalia. He agreed, in 2017, with Sudanese President *al-Bashir,* a lease on an island in the Red Sea for a future military base. This island lies within the border triangle of *Hayaleb,* which is subject to a territorial dispute between Sudan and Egypt. The island of *Suakin,* a former Ottoman possession, was once a relay for pilgrims on the road to Mecca. Suakin is a part of history that the Turkish president would probably like to resurrect in order to compete with Saudi Arabia's tourist industry. Turkey is now territorially also in a strong position in Syria after the U.S.'s unilateral disengagement.

Additionally, Turkey broke the Saudi-sponsored blockade on Qatar by shipping goods through its military base in Qatar. Through bilateral agreements, President Erdoğan sent Turkish troops to protect Qatar from Gulf countries contemplating any potential military aggression. Turkey is NATO's second-largest military power; coupled with its sophisticated diplomatic and intelligence services, it has enough ability to protect and support Qatar and offers the *al-Thani* family a minor yet functional alternative to American protection. This support has paid dividends: Qatar has invested more than $20 billion in the Turkish economy and premium media influence on its *Al Jazeera* channel.

Another most significant change in Turkish policy is the current pivot toward Iran and Russia. President Erdoğan's worldview shares many similarities with those of *Ali Khamenei* and *Vladimir Putin*. In addition, the potential for an Ottoman/Persian axis would catch the West completely by surprise and constitute an absolute game changer—a most original **counter-opening** on the chessboard.

Like Tehran and Moscow, Ankara, at least in the media, like Iran, is now more anti-Western than at any point in recent history. The modern, secular Turkish Republic, which rose from the remnants of the Ottoman Empire, is home to dozens of opposition Arab news channels and thousands of Muslim Brotherhood members. President Erdoğan has supported the Muslim Brotherhood across the Arab world since the 2011 revolutions of the Arab Spring. Turkey has turned into a favorite hub for Islamist dissidents from across the Arab world. Pro-western media is curtailed or silenced. Any dissident voice is crushed within days—the three countries share a visceral dislike for criticism.

Although Turkey's leadership has also become a vociferous champion of traditional Muslim causes, such as a Palestinian state, and newer causes, such as the *Rohingyas* in *Myanmar*, the traditional cries of *"Death to the West"* in Iran and in Turkey are more media-driven identification banners than real threats. Ankara and Tehran are now enjoying the prominent political position of being the anti-Israel champions—again, in my opinion, more of a unifying brand than a real military threat to Israel. Turkey and Israel, just like Israel and Iran, also enjoy a long history of cooperation and trade.

As mentioned, the Middle East has the potential to suddenly flare up. However, the rallying chants, propaganda cries, and the "war winds" created for public and media consumption are part of a common script across the area. In the face of the feeling of tenuous peace that this script attempts to evoke, the Israeli-Turkish-Iranian dynamic might be the most stable and predictable element in the Middle East.

Turkey's and Iran's weak economies are too reliant on peace, Western partners, and Arab markets to pick massive brawls. Military retaliations are limited in scope and magnitude to the effects they have on the psyche of domestic audiences and securing borders, as in the case of Turkey's advance in Northern Syria and Iran's actions in Syria and Iraq.

Turkey, just like Iran and Egypt, will not commit the full might of its military forces until it perceives the threat to be "existential," meaning an infringement on its territorial integrity and its right to self-determination.

These three are nations which are thousands of years old. A constant reliance on the lessons of their enduring history allows them to feel that political leadership, although important, is transitory and, therefore, expendable and that time is on their side.

There was no chance that Iran would retaliate militarily against the USA when one of its national heroes, *Qasem Soleimani*, head of the Quds forces, was assassinated. There is also no way that a lack of full military retaliation means a change in strategic policy and behavior. *Qasem Soleimani*, just like any other Iranian political and military figure, was expendable. Iran is not. Soleimani is now more useful as an historical figure—a martyr—than as a military commander.

Shooting a bunch of missiles at an almost-empty American base is not a military retaliation; it was executed for domestic consumption. There are plenty of American soft targets that could be taken out by

Iran. But why would Iran ever do it? The historical endgame is what the rook is focused on—a time to fight will come, but it might not be during this century.

The nuisance of *Pasdaran's* fast boats circling around American destroyers in the Strait of Hormuz is not to be considered military operations and tactics; they are content for media reels aimed at the domestic public, in Iran. The American public should stop being gullible and believing that Iran wages war like America does. If an American destroyer swats at the mosquitos, the image of burning Persian vessels is a bigger victory for the Iranian regime than punching a hole in an American vessel. Sinking a few Persian fast boats is no significant military victory for America. The deck is stacked against the Queen in the Hormuz massive movie set.

Turkey is more militarily reactive than Iran because it can afford to be. It is less politically isolated than Iran, and its position within NATO still affords Ankara a range of motion that few Muslim countries possess.

For many centuries, Turkey and Iran have peacefully coexisted with competition and cooperation occurring persistently in many different forms. Turkey and Iran have never been overtly hostile toward each other, but, at the same time, they have never formed a strategic partnership.

Geopolitical location, history, and strategic goals are factors influencing the roles Turkey and Iran play in the world. Over the past few decades, Turkey and Iran's relationship has experienced few unexpected developments despite significant ideological differences.

While fluctuating within a defined range, this *bishop-rook* relationship has proven to be the most consistent and predictable in the Middle East. After a small division at the start of the Syria crisis, the rule of common interests prevailed. Their ability to compartmentalize relations allowed for bilateral cooperation even while engaging in a proxy war in Syria and competing in Iraq. However, there are limitations as to how close they can become, given different political regimes, the traditional Sunni/Shia divide, conflicting geopolitical ambitions, and susceptibilities to "Great Power" influence.

As stated, neither Iran nor Turkey view the other as an existential threat, but they perceive potential rapprochement between remaining regional powers like Saudi Arabia, Egypt, Israel, and UAE as a serious risk.

Turkey and Iran's cooperation intensifies when controversies strain Turkey's bonds with the U.S. and NATO and when U.S. policies favor Israel, Saudi Arabia, and the Syrian Kurds.

Russia is exploiting this opportunity to pull Turkey closer. As Turkey and Iran struggle to improve their economies, trade policy plays as an important instrument in advancing their relationship, as their economies are similar and complementary.

Even during periods of close relations with the U.S., Turkey has been unable to ignore Iran and has opportunistically disobeyed sanctions by exporting goods in exchange for Iranian oil. Under the U.S. *"maximum pressure"* policy on Iran, Turkey faces new trade challenges. Turkey and Iran appear united in opposition to the U.S. and publicly express determination to preserve economic cooperation and the right to self-determination.

Aside from trade, relations between Turkey and Iran are stable along other regional issues of mutual concern. Their participation in the Astana Process brought them closer. The Astana Process talks, held in the capital of Kazakhstan (*Nur-Sultan/Astana*) between 2017 and 2019, resulted in an agreement between Iran, Russia, and Turkey to form a joint monitoring body to work to enforce the UN Resolution 2254 ceasefire in Syria. Turkey and Iran also share a similar position on the Gulf Cooperation Council (GCC) rift, on Kurdish aspirations, on Iraq's future, on Israeli meddling in Azerbaijan, and on the Palestinian cause.

Their stances diverge in some cases, but they find a common thread in the public disapproving of U.S. actions. This alignment allows Russia to expand its clout among the two countries. As best witnessed in northern Syria, the influence and foreign-policy objectives of larger and dominant powers—either the U.S. or Russia—frequently dictate their own policies, leaving them with only limited options.

Turkey and Iran's relationship can be divided into two different but closely associated areas—economy/trade and regional policy.

Turkey's primary reason for having an economic relationship with Iran stems from its desire to diversify energy sources. For several decades, Turkey has relied on Russia for gas imports. But since 1979, Turkey has started to increase gas imports from Iran despite U.S. sanctions against Iran. Even if energy trade has helped reconcile their differences, it has not always been smooth. Over the years, Turkey and Iran have argued over contract terms. Turkey would negotiate for lower prices, while Iran would redirect gas for domestic consumption during harsh winters.

Turkey tried to partner in South Pars field, which Iran shared with Qatar, but when large international companies gave up on the project, Turkey reluctantly followed suit. The project failed because foreign investors were prohibited from having an equity interest in Iranian-owned energy sites.

Despite their disagreement over gas prices, trade between Turkey and Iran continued to increase as Turkey's growing economy demanded more energy. Turkey required a diverse and secure mix of energy producers to ensure stability and low cost. If Turkey loses a major energy supplier, Turkish utility companies and refineries face higher energy costs and shortages. Despite U.S. and U.N. sanctions imposed on Iran in 2011, Turkey continued to import oil and gas from Iran. To circumvent these sanctions, Turkey planned to use gold reserves held at a Turkish bank that had strong ties with the Iranian Republican Guard.

Expanding on this, historical trade with Iran is impossible to disrupt. Embargoes do not work, or, better, they work only during the initial stages. There is never full executive consensus on policies. U.S.-sponsored embargoes are constantly covertly challenged not only by Russia and China but also by America's Arab allies.

Whether it takes place with Turkey or with emirates across the pond, Iranian trade continues. For example, the Omani-Iranian historical links prescind U.S. foreign policy in the area; so do the strong ties between the Dubai merchant classes and the Persian market.

When touring the *Gold Souk* in *Deira*, while tourists are negotiating on merchandise, one should take a little stroll through the *Old Souk* to the banks of the Dubai Creek and marvel at the large number of *dhows,* filled to perilous levels by white goods and products of any kind, waiting to sail. The crews are more than forthcoming when, over a sweet Arabic *chai*, you ask them where they are headed: "*Bilad Faris*" say the captains. "*Fars*" say the Urdu-speaking crews ("We are going to Iran").

Different souk, same feeling. In Oman, a Sunni sultanate, the *Mutrah Souk* in Muscat is right next to the Shia Quarter. The historical quarter is discreetly guarded by unarmed citizens who are friendly and who allow tourists with Italian accents to tour this historical Iranian foothold across the pond. The quarter is right next to the *Masjid Al Rasool Al A'dham* Shia mosque, which is merely a testimony to the Persian legacy of *Maka* (later *Mazun*), a satrapy of the Achaemenid Empire of Persia, well in the Pre-Islamic period. The same Pre-Islamic ties can be found in Bahrain (which is one of the earlier Western inventions in the Gulf), when Britain certified the legitimacy to rule of the Sunni *Al Khalifa* family over a majority Shia population largely groomed, a few centuries before, by the *Shah Abbas I* of the Persian Safavid dynasty.

Despite the many public announcements of yet more maximum-pressure sanctions initiative against Iran, in which America vows to close all loopholes that Iran had previously exploited, making it more difficult for countries to continue trading with Iran, the embargo will never be watertight and biting as the public opinion is allowed to believe.

Furthermore, because of historical pressures against the Iranian oil economy, that rook has geared its economy to absorb the shock of a dramatic reduction in oil sales. This is not to say that oil sales aren't an important pillar of the Iranian economy but a warning that a drastic fall in oil prices or an over-supply of crude is likely to damage more the economies of the pro-U.S. bloc than its Iranian foe.

The Syrian quagmire is perhaps the best example of the inherent paradox which is the Middle Eastern chessboard. Turkish and Iranian relations were strained after the outbreak of the Syrian war. While Iran staunchly supported the Syrian regime, Turkey was one of the main benefactors of opposition against the regime. Turkey, a NATO member and U.S. ally, had permitted extremist groups to use its territory. Turkey also acted in a duplicitous manner and often demonstrated a reluctance to take on ISIS directly while instead preferring to focus on fighting the Kurds, a U.S. ally. Iran, the main U.S. foe in the region, kept pounding ISIS, the foe of the U.S.-led coalition, in both Iraq and Syria, using its *Quds* forces and *Hezbollah* proxies. Israel kept pounding *Hezbollah* positions in Syria, which were defending against ISIS attacks aimed at consolidating a foothold from which to hit Damascus, Beirut, and…. Israel.

In early March 2016, at a time when Turkey-Russia relations were at a low point, Russia's U.N. Security Council Representative presented evidence alleging Turkey's illegal oil trade with ISIS and the *al-Nusra Front* terrorist organization, but when the coup d'état failed to overthrow the Turkish government in 2016, Russia and Iran were almost alone in supporting Erdoğan. In the region, the U.S. withdrawal from Syria and the assassination of the Quds commander, Qasem Soleimani, have been compared to Britain's 1968 *East of Suez* retreat, which signaled the formal changing of the guard, as a *Queen* piece, between Britain and the United States of America.

Is the American retreat from Syria one of the pivotal moves in the history of the Middle Eastern chess game? Too soon to say. As mentioned in the introduction, the Middle East short-term moves and seismic geopolitical consequences do not have the same correlations that we witness in the rest of the world. Which country could be the Queen in the short term anyway? It is difficult to see, in today's world, a country that could replace the United States as the alternative superpower. Later, in the chapter dedicated to the knights, we shall go into further details.

The West's Bishop
Israel

L'Shana Haba'ah B'Yerushalayim
(Next Year in Jerusalem)*

*Hebrew phrase commonly recited during
Passover Seder and the Ne'ila service on Yom
Kippur. It was initially a diaspora tradition,
but it is now common everywhere.

THIS MIGHT BE THE MOST difficult subject in the entire book. Thousands upon thousands of books have been written about the subject, and opinions vary dramatically, but they are all guaranteed to evoke strong feelings and bipartisanship.

Writing about Israel usually evokes reactions, strong passions, and opinions on a global scale. Polarized passions on the Jewish/Zionist/Israeli reality mean that the very mention of opinions, pro or counter the Jewish state, can guarantee that the author is branded as a dirty Zionist, a supporter of war criminals, by one side, or anti-semitic, by the other.

There are plenty of human tragedies that still evoke profound sorrow among parties, like the Armenian genocide, Rwanda's massacre of *Tutsis*, the ethnic cleansing in Kosovo and Bosnia, the *Shoah* (the *Holocaust*), and the massacres of Arab villagers perpetrated by Jewish militia, to name a few. Of all the massacres and genocides which have been perpetrated in the history of man, the Shoah is the genocide that has been portrayed the most because it affected the coreligionists of one of the most powerful social strata in the world.

Even if contextualized, the consequences of all of these senseless acts of violence should be addressed and never allowed to be forgotten. All massacres and genocides should have their Nuremberg and their *Simon Wiesenthals*. If the world was a just place, all those historical moments which have resulted in great loss of life and human displacement should be addressed and healed.

Those episodes, which have not been yet addressed by independent bodies tasked to enforce accountability in an impartial and decisive manner, are a guarantee of prolonged strife, to which no permanent solution can be provided. **History is a testimony that unhealed memories last forever.**

Human beings need safety, justice, and closure before they need economic reparations. In the long term, there is no price tag for the loss of a loved one or your cherished memories. Substitute a human being's loving memory with a painful one, and you might pay for it with the loss of your own peace. When it comes to this terrible consequence, the children of the Shoah should be our teachers.

When analyzing the creation of the State of Israel, even when faced with documentary reality, it is difficult to settle on a commonly accepted narrative. There are many arguments from both sides of the aisle, but five vital matters need to be metabolized:

First, albeit the result of a Zionist endeavor, Israel is a Western and, most importantly, a Christian creation—a plan which was more emotional and political, rather than strategic. Jewish power and influence alone would not have been enough to establish the reality of a Jewish state. The creation of the State of Israel was yet another foreign-policy initiative aimed at the national domestic audiences of Christian nations.

Second, the Israeli policy of partition, annexation, and land appropriation in the Holy Land is illegal. It might be caused by legitimate security concerns, but it is still illegal, in today's age.

Third, the biggest threat to Israel's survival is not a militant Arab insurrection but myopic 'black-and-white' policies which are unwilling to consider that terrorism is terrorism (whether perpetrated by Palestinians or by Jews) and that it has origins in the memory of the bloodshed caused, by both sides, a century ago. A bloodshed that, by being perpetuated, shall see no end, ever.

Fourth, Israel might be the Zionist dream of legitimacy, independence, and autonomy, but it keeps functioning as the West's outpost against militant Pan-Arabism. It might be a Jewish homeland, but it is, at the end of the day, just a Western bishop in the way it operates and in the way it is perceived by the vast majority of Middle Easterners.

Fifth, at this stage, just as it is said of its nemesis Iran, Israel needs to decide whether it is a state of international law or a religious cause.

As an avid reader of history books on Islamic imperialism, I came to accept that all modern Arabs reach back to their history to dictate their current behavior and policies. After all, when you talk to any Arab or Persian, it seems like their time never went by. They talk about something that happened during the Crusades as if it had happened yesterday.

Christian consciousness in Europe, Africa, and Asia is no different. Whether in Europe, Kenya, or modern *Outremer*, Christians' memory is not shorter than the Muslims'.

The same applies to the Jewish people, wherever they live and prosper.

The Islamist problem had come too close to home for Europeans' cultural heritage to forget. If you find this difficult to comprehend, just ask European Roman Catholics, Libyan and Egyptian Copts, Iraqi Assyrians, and Armenian Orthodox.

I feel the need to further qualify what I mean by "Christian Europe." I believe that modern Europe is both secular and multicultural.

Even in countries where a conservative right is dominant, there generally is little appetite for Christian (whether Catholic or Protestant) attitude toward sex, abortion, or women rights.

Even if the modern Roman Catholic church is softening its stance considerably, in the attempt to re-assert a Christian Europe, the continent is staying secular. What I mean by "Christian Europe" is the historical reality which constitutes the foundations of the continent's Judeo-Christian cultural heritage and which was subjected to Islamic invasions and massacres. Too many Turkish and Saracen massacres have been perpetrated, across Europe, to be easily forgotten.

By that, I am not attempting to justify the massacres that were perpetrated by Christian Crusaders in the Holy Land. I am merely stating that if Arabs still have a beef with 'Crusaders,' so do the Europeans with the 'Moors.'

It is in this context that the warning words of theologians and statesmen like Saint Isidore of Seville have to be considered, as they shaped what the leadership of Western powers believed were the appropriate policies aimed at emasculating Islamist imperialism—military interventions, state creations, partitions, before and after taking down the Ottoman caliphate, in 1918.

Saint Isidore of Seville was a Spanish monk and completely unfamiliar with the Islamic conquest of the Holy Land. What he witnessed was the slow but steady infiltration by North African Moors in the Iberian Peninsula and the forced subjugation of Christian believers, most of whom were sold into slavery. Saint Isidore died before he could see the entire south of Spain (Andalus) taken over by the Moors but left a few fateful words about just war: *"A war is just when it is carried on after a declaration to recover property or repel enemies—there is a war between Christians and Moors, and there will be until the Christians have recovered their lands that the Moors have taken from them by force."*

The loss of Roman Catholic Southern Spain to the Muslim Moors might have stung Christian consciousness more than the loss of the

Orthodox Byzantine empire to the Turks, as the Western Christians had come to see themselves as separate from their Eastern brethren. Speaking to any Middle Easterner, one shall hear the consensus that the subsequent loss of Andalus to the Roman Catholic Spanish Christian *Reconquista,* in 1236, had stunned the Muslim world more than the losses at Tours, Vienna, and Lepanto.

Losses to infidels' armies are not widely reported in school textbooks across the Islamic world, but the shrinking territory, with the loss of prestige and status, are widely used to warn of the consequences that leaving the pious path of Allah and failing to abide by Mohammed's teachings can provide.

Fully five centuries later, in 1977, Egypt's then-Foreign Minister *Boutros Boutros-Ghali,* while talking to his Israeli counterpart, *Moshe Dayan,* stated: *"Palestine is (for us) a sore spot, and we are still mourning the loss of Andalus..."* Boutros-Ghali recalls the conversation in his book *Egypt's Road to Jerusalem—A Diplomat's Story of the Struggle for Peace in the Middle East.*

Spiritual Pan-Arabism, as a cultural awakening which furthers artistic, scientific, and economic progress, is of no threat to the world—it is a gift to humankind. Militant Islamist Pan-Arabism, with its theological distortions and aberrant application of draconian Sharia law, is a threat to the world.

Alan G. Jamieson, author of *Faith and Sword—A Short History of Christian-Muslim Conflict,* eloquently states: *"In all the long centuries of Christian-Muslim conflict, never has the military imbalance between the two sides been greater, yet the dominant West can apparently derive no comfort from the fact that a still-swinging scimitar will always overcome a strong but sheathed sword."*

The continued existence of the State of Israel guarantees that America's sword will not stay sheathed. America is home to the world's wealthiest and most powerful Jewish community. The common belief amongst Middle Eastern operators is that, despite the historical criticism of the way the Israel was created, most of the West **emotionally** needs the State of Israel to exist as much as most of the Jewish people do. Islamists have capitalized on it and used it to their propaganda advantage.

The Islamists' perception of the American-Israel partnership is one of a Crusader's power, willing to spill the blood of innocents to protect the Jewish Zionists' crimes. Salafi and Wahhabi rhetoric is full of references to this belief.

There are three main declarations of holy war that are at the base of today's Islamist Jihad. Bin Laden's 1996 *fatwā* is sometimes called the *Ladenese epistle*.

In it, Bin Laden stated: *"It is not concealed from you that the people of Islam had suffered from aggression, iniquity, and injustice imposed on them by the Jewish-Christian alliance and their collaborators to the extent that the Muslims' blood became the cheapest and their wealth and assets looted by the hands of the enemies. Their blood was spilled in Palestine and Iraq. The horrifying pictures of the massacre of Qana, in Lebanon, are still fresh in our memory... Muslims became aware that they were the main targets of the Jewish-Crusader alliance of aggression."*

In 1998, similar reasons were contained in two other declarations, one by Bin Laden and other four regional Islamist leaders, and one by the World Islamic Front statement titled *"Jihad Against Jews and Crusaders."* Most statements echo Bin Laden's view that *"The Americans' aims behind these wars are religious and economic; the aim is also to serve the Jews' petty state and divert attention from its occupation of Jerusalem* and *murder of Muslims there. The best proof of this is their eagerness to destroy Iraq, the strongest neighboring Arab state, and their endeavor to fragment all the states of the region such as Iraq, Saudi Arabia, Egypt, and Sudan into paper statelets and through their disunion and weakness to guarantee Israel's survival and the continuation of the brutal crusade occupation of the Peninsula."*

Bin Laden might be dead, and so might all the signatories of these declarations of war, but the sentiment is still prevalent all over the Middle East and in the rest of the Muslim world. U.S. inaction with regard to the Israeli annexation of the West Bank play into the Islamists' narrative.

Regional militant Pan-Arabism might be a limited threat to the rest of the world, but it is an existential threat to Israel. The only party that can truly mitigate that risk is Israel itself, but it will not be able to do so through military action and land grabbing. Jews have been fighting in that land for the past 4000 years. There is no indication that it could change.

Therefore, I believe that, in the absence of rational solutions to the diatribe, for the time being, any serious attempts at reviving militant Pan-Arabism, like those of secular Gamal Abdel Nasser or the Jihadi vision of Abu Bakr Al-Baghdadi will continue to be met with Western military, economic, and political action.

For the next century, I forecast that no Pan-Arabic dream is destined to succeed, no matter what the Islamist perception of the West's current weakness might be.

In his *Digest of the Middle East*, the British-American historian Bernard Lewis, one of the best-known Oriental-history experts, stated: *"The Middle East is not a geographical region; rather it is a concept that is based upon Western orientation to the world."*

Modern Israel dates back about a century since the British government issued the Balfour Declaration, in 1917. The Zionist efforts to claim a land for the Jews became a mighty political wave that had unlikely supporters in Germany's National Socialist Party and unlikely detractors like the defense departments, intelligence agencies, and foreign-affairs ministries of the countries which eventually pulled the trigger on the creation of the Jewish state in 1948—the USA, Great Britain, and France. In these three countries, the political leaderships overruled the recommendations of their foreign-affairs experts for the sake of domestic-policy support from the powerful national Zionist movements.

Alison Weir, in her book *Against Our Better Judgement—The hidden history of how the U.S. was used to create Israel,* documents the claims that the creation of Israel was what would drag the USA into policing the Middle East as long as Israel exists. Her book is 229 pages long. She takes only 93 pages to espouse her theory; the rest are supporting sources, references, and documentation. Despite backing every single statement of hers with several reputable sources, she has still been branded as antisemitic.

Israel is a nuclear nation—the only Middle Eastern nuclear country. It is because of this and the assured backing of the West that it can claim the role of a bishop on the chessboard. Israel could independently be a very powerful regional actor. At present, it is not; its power is primarily a reflection of American power in the region, but it is isolated by choice. Since 1948, Israel has gotten stronger, more organized, richer, and more stable. However, it still lacks economic independence, population size, and the global credibility of a powerhouse.

Furthermore, its neighbors have grown, too, maybe not economically, but in population size and military strength. Even *Hezbollah* is no longer just a nuisance.

Genuine alliances between Israel and Arab states are just a myth. There might be economic and security cooperation or temporary alignment on minor policy matters, but the prospect of a true alliance between Israel and any Arab state is as likely as the hardliner conservative Christians' acceptance of Christ's tomb being protected by Jewish soldiers.

There is a common allegorical tale, which originated at the time of Egypt's overture toward Israel, that still gets recounted around the Arab world. It is the story of the mother with many children who suddenly leaves her home, children, and responsibilities to go off with a *khawagah* (foreigner). The children wail and rebel against their mother, accusing her of treachery and treason. In the original story, the mother was meant to be Egypt and the *khawagah* Israel. Since 1948, no Arab nation has truly willed to be that mother, whether with ambitions to be a leading nation among Arabs or not.

Israel could change the way it is perceived in the region, but it will not be able to accomplish that unless it truly becomes a Middle Eastern nation. Until then, it will always be what the other countries in the Middle East believe it is—a *khawagah,* a Western creation, a foreign occupier.

Even within those Arab countries which do not care too much for the Palestinians, which have normalized relations with Israel and have finally accepted the reality of Israel's permanence, when diplomacy language gets put aside, they resort to the usual narrative of the Israelis as an array of outsiders—foreigners from Europe and Asia who have stolen land that belongs to Middle Easterners and all in the name of exclusive religious rights that are a cover-up for a crime that keeps going unpunished. We are in the presence, they say, of a theological charade, given that those powers that claim to uphold justice around the world but keep protecting the crime are not even Jewish but Christian.

It might take two or three centuries for the successors of the original Israeli settlers to start being considered as locals.

There is another very frequent assertion which, as Zhou Enlai's, might have been misattributed or taken in a different context. It was initially, perhaps mistakenly, attributed to Golda Meir, a giant of Israel's history: *"Peace will come when the Arabs will love their children more than they hate us."*

It is more complicated than that. Peace will come when the Palestinians will be able to give their children what they believe is a suitable home, not what the Israelis believe is a suitable home. When one has no home, one has little to lose. **Once you have lost yourself and your honor, death does not look that horrifying and might become a glorious alternative.**

There is no economic reparation within the Middle East Peace Process that can address the pain caused in the years around Israel's creation. That period and its lasting consequences need to be addressed in a responsible manner, without unnecessary bribes financed by countries that are perceived as interested outsiders.

All the Middle Eastern countries that were summoned to the June 2019 Manama Economic Summit showed the Queen what the West has come to believe is merely a hollow act of deference and typical Arab duplicity—all smiles and nods and, behind the back, criticism and sneering.

What the West believes is duplicity is a form of Oriental courtesy to please the outsiders in the absence of trust and clarity of intent. The Arabs feel that *The Deal of the Century* is merely a brand. American administrations change every eight years at the most, and a consistent policy cannot be expected. The only constant to be expected is America's absolute support for Israel. This is what they have witnessed since 1948, therefore, they feel that the Queen will never be an honest broker, no matter whether the administration is led by a Democrat or a Republican.

Jerusalem is not a city. It is a dream, a concept. So is Rome. These two cities have ceased being geographical places and have become symbols. Rome might be in Italy, and people might think of Italy and think of Rome, but, as it is the site of the Holy See, it does not belong only to the Italians; it belongs to humanity. Italians are entrusted as Rome's custodians and should cherish and take care of it while facilitating free access to all those who want to visit and participate in its glory. Jerusalem is the same. It ceased being exclusively Jewish in 70 AD. Since then, every time a religious faction has laid an absolute claim to it, it has resulted in strife and bloodshed. Jerusalem does not belong only to the Israelis or to the Palestinians, as a matter of fact, it belongs to humanity. *The Kingdom of Heaven* belongs to the three Abrahamic faiths.

This point is immortalized in a fictional scene of the movie *Kingdom of Heaven* (2005). Balian of Ibelin, the last Crusader commander of Jerusalem, has just surrendered the city to *Salah-ad-Din*, the legendary Kurdish commander of the Muslim forces. He points to the many deaths that had occurred during the siege and asks the enemy leader: *"What is Jerusalem worth?"* *"Nothing…"* responds the Muslim fighter—*"and everything."*

Jerusalem is *everything* to many, irrespective of where they live. It is where our faith resides. It is no longer just a territory; it is a piece of our soul. It belongs to my Jewish, Christian, and Muslim brothers and sisters, all over the world. Whether we are just splinters of the Jewish faith or not, we are all *People of the Book.* Since we were all little children, we were thought that *Yerushalayim, Golghota,* and *Quds* was the place where everything started (Jews and Christians) and ended (Muslims). *L'Shana Haba'ah B'Yerushalayim,* "Next year in Jerusalem," applies to all of us. Israel cannot ignore this.

Claiming sole ownership of Jerusalem will not make this need go away. Children will be taught of their loss for many more centuries. History teaches that physical (and geographical) possessions can be transitory. Oneness seems to be the only thing which is eternal.

Roman Catholic Cardinal *Fernando Filoni* is the former *Nunzio Apostolico,* the Vatican Ambassador, to Jordan and Iraq.

While in Iraq, Filoni defended the freedom of the Catholic Church under the regime of Saddam Hussein and, in line with the Pope's position, opposed the U.S.-led invasion of the country in 2003. He remained in Baghdad as American bombs fell, which he called "nothing exceptional."

After the fall of Saddam, he recognized the newfound freedom enjoyed by the people, but he warned against the lack of security and the slow development of the economy. He expressed mixed feelings toward the new constitution, which he described as both a *"positive step toward normalization in the country"* and *"contradictory in some areas,"* and supported the peaceful coexistence between Christians and Muslims.

More fortunate than his fellow diplomat Vieira de Mello, Filoni came close to being killed in Baghdad on 1 February 2006, when a car bomb exploded next to the *nunciature* (the Vatican embassy). He served in Iraq and Jordan until 25 February 2006.

Pope Francis named him Grand Master of the *Equestrian Order of the Holy Sepulchre of Jerusalem* on 8 December 2019. The Order is a lay institution placed under the protection of the Holy See. Its main aim is to strengthen among its members the practice of Christian life, to sustain and aid the charitable, cultural, and social works and institutions of the Catholic Church in the Holy Land, particularly those of the Latin Patriarchate of Jerusalem, which also includes Cyprus and Jordan, thus supporting the Christian presence in the Lands of the Bible.

In his Lenten (March) 2020 letter to the members of the Order, he stated: *".... offering assistance to the Holy Land and to its human, cultural, and spiritual institutions, and serving the Church and the Communities living there in respect of the fundamental human rights, while favoring dialogue between diverse peoples and promoting peace. Jesus reminds us that the promoters of peace, the peacemakers, will be called children of God..."*

Adding to Cardinal Filoni's message of unity among *"diverse people,"* local studies suggest that the root of resentment is not only a matter of religion; it is primarily a matter of habitat and heritage.

According to the report *"Is Peace Possible?"* by the Justice and Peace Commission of the Assembly of Catholic Ordinaries in the Holy Land, the Christian Palestinian diaspora identifies itself more with its Muslim neighbors than with Western Christians. The general observation is that their Western co-religionists do not share their heritage and ancestry, therefore, they attempt to believe that protecting stones—buildings and monuments—is the equivalent of protecting people. When I visited The Church of the Holy Sepulchre, I was left with the feeling that the place meant more to Christian pilgrims than to local Christians. The same goes for the Saint Peter Basilica and most of the Romans.

Considering this need of all people of the Abrahamic faith to connect with the land, what are the available political solutions?

A two-state solution that respects free access to the sites of wor-ship might be possible but only if it addresses the reasons that this political settlement is needed. If *Hamas* and *Fatah* are terrorist orga-nizations, so were the *Haganah*, the *Stern Gang*, and the *Irgun*. Until the first two factions continue to be considered terrorists, while the other three are celebrated as freedom fighters, there will be no healing and no true middle ground. To my historical recollection, the last three organizations preceded the creation of the first two. Since the fall of the Ottoman Empire, the first-ever terrorist organizations in the Holy Land have been Jewish rather than Muslim. Healing starts with accountability.

Israel has much to give to the entire region. It is the home of great people, great minds who can help make the region prosperous and peaceful. As the original people of the Abrahamic monotheistic faith, Israelis could undoubtedly be the extraordinary example of industri-ousness, forgiveness, peace, and amalgamation, all in the name of a common interfaith dream. There are no chosen people. The God of Abraham is a wholly inclusive one. He is a God of peace, not of war.

I have faith that Israel can take the lead and represent hope and the living proof that anything is possible despite enormous tragedies and setbacks, because Israel can be the entire world's wall against injustice and political opportunism.

The Knights
China and Russia

"My notion of the KGB came
from romantic spy stories.

"I was a pure and utterly successful
product of Soviet patriotic education."
Vladimir Putin

"Superpowers have a lot of room for error.
Unlike lesser nations, they can shrug off many
of the consequences of failed policies. Their
weight and influence can compensate for
subpar statecraft. But bad policy eventually
takes its toll on everyone. And right now, bad
policy is taking its toll on the United States."
Hal Brands—Foreign Affairs—*September 2019*

I N A PERIOD WHEN America is re-evaluating its need for continued involvement in the Middle East, China and Russia's presence in that area of the world is regarded as an obligation by both Beijing and Moscow, because it is seen as existential.

China, which is currently on the edge of an economic precipice, is constantly seeking markets to exploit because of its great reliance on foreign energy sources and to keep the giant *Renminbi* manipulation going. Access to markets guarantees that China's *house of cards* will continue. China has undertaken a very dangerous leverage bet on constant growth. When China's economy stops, the country will not just stop, it will collapse.

Russia might not be able to rebuild a Union of Soviet Socialist Republics and count on its former power, but, under Vladimir Putin's nostalgic view of history, it is attempting to maximize its current, more-limited resources to *"influence through disruption,"* opting for paramilitary subversion operations and medium-term security-cooperation agreements rather than long-term regional commitments.

For different reasons, neither Russia nor China have the long-term economic muscle to play the role of the *Queen* in the Middle East, nor do they wish to. Yet they play the knights' role on the chessboard. Knights can be nimble raiders, fast, unpredictable marauders, but they have limited reach because they lack either economic or military capacity to dominate the system.

Both countries are stepping up the range of their disruptive tactics, but they seem to be losing the economic confrontation with the Queen. For all of its aggressive posture around the world, Russia's economy is growing at half the pace of the United States', and its dream of becoming an economic superpower is quickly fading. Also, despite all alarmist reports of a Chinese economic takeover, it was America that experienced a true economic golden decade. China's plan to provide an alternative to the U.S. dollar as the world's currency has failed.

If it is true that there are some signs of stress in the American economy and in the political scene, it is also true that these signs are stronger in both China and Russia. The world's economy is still U.S.-dollar based, and the American bi-party system, albeit extremely polarized, is in no more danger than Putin's Stalinist tenure or the CCP's (Chinese Communist Party) impending doom.

America's liberal internationalism, given up for dead after the election of Donald Trump, is still alive and kicking. It is still very welcome in the more-progressive areas of the Middle East. China and Russia's inflexible alternative is America's greatest asset.

America's traditional power might not be able to buy the influence and access it once did, but it has quickly adapted to the new, ever-changing messy scenario by creating *ad hoc* arrangements. America clearly does not worry about appearing unreliable in the region.

As mentioned, regional "Great Powers" like these two knights may have internal problems or domestic destabilizing factors. China's weakness might be more predictable than Russia's due to its hyper-leveraged economic-expansion strategy, and it seems to lack the Russian willingness to see its personnel and proxies slaughtered in regional conflicts—*Sun Tzu* wisdom vs *Georgy Konstantinovich Zhukov* suicidal pragmatism.

China's Communist Party is increasingly struggling to keep control of the information among its globalized and no-longer-Communist public. Facing the enormous challenge of keeping its people in line while the tenuous image of national wealth is fading faster than expected, it cannot afford the domestic broadcasting of its soldiers butchered on the streets of a distant Middle Eastern town. The stoic 'immolator for the commune' of Mao Zedong's China no longer exists. Maybe, it never truly existed. Modern Chinese are the most individualistic human beings I have met—which is counter-intuitive for a country of 1.4 billion souls. Human waves ready to self-immolate for the greatness of the People's Republic can no longer be found.

On the other hand, maybe favored by increasing wealth discrepancies and economic woes, Vladimir Putin's Russian vision has the quality of a Stalinist Russia—its people are expendable as ever. Its people still as ready to be killed for the Federation, and, if they are not ready, they can be easily made ready.

In the early months of the German *Unternehmen Barbarossa*, the fight was so exceptionally desperate that the Red Army often found themselves with no alternative but to conduct massed charges with civilians—the *Narodnoe Opolcheniye*. These were civilians pressed into service and thrown against the Germans to buy time. There were not enough rifles, so some of these poor individuals were armed, and some were not. If an armed man or woman would fall, another would pick up his rifle. In some cases, they were forced at gunpoint. Peasants, factory workers, accountants, professors: some had volunteered, or been forced to volunteer, with no medical assistance, no uniforms, no transport, and no supply system.

In Stalingrad, metal workers from the *Barrikady Ordnance Factory*, the *Red October Steel Works* and the *Dzerzhinsky Tractor Factory* were press-ganged into service against professional Axis soldiers. They died in droves. For the Soviet leadership, wasting trained soldiers made little long-term economic or strategic sense.

This disregard for the safety of its people, whether they be security contractors, paramilitary, or military personnel has been demonstrated again and again in Afghanistan, Chechnya, the Ukraine, Crimea, and Syria. It has, so far, saved Russia and made it feared around the world.

Ruthlessness or pragmatism aside, war has a steep cost. These knights no longer have the option of settling disputes with the Queen on the battlefield. Ideology might be important, but, in today's Russia and China, money comes first.

The post-World War II American imperative to counter the spread of Communism in the lands of vast energy resources is no longer an historical reality, given that both oligarchic Russia and plutocratic China might, in their reckless economic races, be even more capitalistic than America, at this stage.

It is important to understand that, even if America's reliance on its own oil and Russia's energy exports have taken the bite out of OPEC's hegemony, the world's energy market is still a very destabilizing factor. A global pandemic or an all-out war to depress oil prices or military instability which could raise them have the ability to wreak havoc around the world. America, whose gross domestic product (GDP) constitutes more than a quarter of the world's GDP, will remain ever watchful of the energy market for the foreseeable future.

In today's Middle East, the conditions that had initially led to U.S. involvement might not have changed regarding Israel's continuous security needs. However, they have morphed in the wake of rising economic rather than ideological competitors, and the Middle East has now become even more of an economic market for competition than just a battlefield.

The most important elements to understand in this competition are the objectives of the major foreign powers and the responses of the regional Middle Eastern states. Russia and China might have different motivations in the Middle East, however, because the U.S. already dominates the region, both Russia and China have common cause in seeking to weaken the Queen's legitimacy. Regional actors' acceptance or rejection of the major powers' policies temporarily tips the balance of power and affects the most important commodity—regional access.

The opportunities for China and Russia in filling voids left by the U.S. occur when America demonstrates less need for regional allies. Those regional chess pieces, when led to question America's sustained commitment, which increases their fear of isolation/abandonment, look elsewhere for support. Therefore, they are more and more likely to resort to multiple hedging alliance strategies, giving space to China and Russia to penetrate. States that feel unprotected hedge their bets with potential suitors. The main currency of exchange is access—both for economic markets and for military cooperation and basing.

Because of the U.S.'s recent calculated retrenchment, China and Russia can access Middle Eastern countries with relative ease, given regional countries' constant need to balance security and development requirements.

A DIME (Diplomatic, Informational, Military, and Economic) analysis suggests that, while Chinese influence is a moderate threat in the short to medium term, Russia currently constitutes a significant challenge to American interests. Russia has already gained "security guarantor" status in Syria and shows willingness to expand its influence through arms sales and security cooperation. On the other hand, China has less interest in shaping the region and challenging the U.S., though it has made significant inroads in the economic and informational domains.

On the diplomatic side, China, and Russia, as with many countries in the Middle East, are often preoccupied with internal stability, territorial integrity, regime survival, and sustaining economic growth. As such, their diplomatic stance on many issues is similar to the preferences of regional actors.

Their diplomatic policy of non-interference in other countries' domestic affairs is generally viewed favorably by Middle Eastern regimes that prize their right to self-determination and that are traditionally reluctant to deal with caveats often attached to U.S. aid—human-rights respect and gender equality. Arabs often tell me that Chinese and Russian aid very rarely comes with conditions attached, unlike aid from the U.S., with conditions that reveal a paternalistic relationship and a lack of understanding of local culture.

I easily reply that, in the Middle East, no foreign aid comes for free. **The real price tag is in the small print, and, culturally, the U.S. tends to use a large print.**

Even if perceived as unconditional, Beijing and Moscow's diplomatic engagements differ in their objectives.

Chinese diplomatic efforts aim to manage conflicts in order to avoid friction for itself, rather than end conflicts. Beijing has captured the attention of many developing countries in the region through an approach that pragmatically links diplomacy, commerce, aid, and economic investment. Although Chinese diplomatic engagements take heed not to confront the U.S., China endeavors to erode American legitimacy by positioning itself as an honest broker on issues that the U.S. might have failed to address.

On the other hand, the geographical proximity allows Russia to oppose the U.S.'s regional preferences. Moscow has a pragmatic approach, which facilitates multilateral dialogue with all stakeholders. Avoiding interventions, Russia strongly opposes the value-based policies of the West. Because of its strategic military capabilities and influence on international organizations, Russia has the power to support actors that the Western nations do not support.

For Moscow, diplomacy is a domain that enhances the effects of its military capabilities. Russia considers spoiling the existing diplomatic mechanisms and creating alternative ones as a cheap and effective method to erode U.S. influence and emerge as a reliable partner to the regional states. In addition, Moscow's worldwide diplomatic presence helps Russia portray an image as a major power and galvanize domestic support to the administration.

In the informational sector, Chinese information efforts are penetrating the region. China's Communist Party's leveraged bet has achieved the illusion of growth through a quasi-capitalist market and, without (so far) losing the grip over the population, has significantly discredited the Western "development through democratization" theories. This illusion provides an alternative, non-democratic model for development that is convenient for many leaders in the Middle East.

Moreover, China gains advantage by staying neutral toward values such as human rights. It refrains from conducting foreign policy based on ideology. Unlike Western democracies, China accepts regime types as domestic preferences and does not impose any type of stipulation to further the relations. This approach exposes the U.S. as an interventionist state that does not respect the international order. The U.S. has a complex domestic political system, within which the branches of the state have different approaches to foreign policy.

Usually, the executive branch has a more pragmatic approach to the region, while the legislative branch has a more value-centric approach, either of which may predominate at any time. Yet, ordinary people in the Middle East tend to think of the U.S. as a singular and rigid political entity with centralized decision-making. Therefore, regional public opinion generally believes that America is not loyal to its proclaimed values or commitments and that it uses "values" as an excuse to meddle in the domestic affairs of regional countries.

Also, China appears as a strong supporter of stability. It avoids potential chaos in the region, because it may adversely affect its own interests in terms of energy security, economic welfare, and trade revenue. Alternatively, regional states view U.S. hints at encouraging regime change as highly destabilizing. Even though the U.S. continues to pursue diplomacy, international assistance programs, and economic and informational exchange, they remain ineffective because, ultimately, it is the U.S. policies that generate anger and antipathy in the region.

Russia is attempting to dominate the informational domain by conveying two fundamental messages: First, the West does not respect national sovereignty, and its actions are self-motivated. Second, since Moscow's ability to shape political outcomes is limited, the unipolar world is undesirable, and multi-polarity is preferable.

On the economic side, since the mid-1990s, rapid economic growth is vital for the Chinese regime for several reasons, above all for social stability in the country and for regime survival. Beijing's economic interests constitute the most dominant factor in determining its foreign policy toward the Middle East. It focuses on stability to ensure uninterrupted access to natural resources, trade, and commercial relations. Chinese firms have contracted billions of dollars for construction, infrastructure, and technology in the region.

For Russia, the Middle East is a venue for counteracting economic isolation and sanctions. In addition, Russia seeks to export its arms, nuclear technology, and investment to key locations to control the flow of energy as a strategic tool of influence. Both Russia and China are increasingly eager to challenge the U.S. dollar's economic supremacy. They regard the American national currency as the extension of U.S. political influence and seek ways and means to overcome this supremacy.

China is highly dependent on regional energy resources. Concurrently, it needs stability for uninterrupted trade and resource flow. Therefore, it naturally opposes U.S. sanctions against Iran, which has become a major thorn for Washington policymakers. On the other hand, Russia is a major hydrocarbon-exporting country that is keen to implement aggressive energy policies aimed at ensuring monopoly, especially vis-à-vis Europe.

This dominant position prevents European countries from imposing harsher sanctions on Moscow. Therefore, Moscow considers controlling the "direction of energy flow" as a key strategic objective and tool. Nonetheless, newly discovered natural-gas resources in the Eastern Mediterranean Sea add significant complications to its objectives, which explains why Russia currently pursues active diplomacy to position itself in and around all stakeholders. Indeed, Moscow has already developed special relations with Egypt, Israel, Lebanon, Cyprus, Palestine, and even Libya. From this perspective, it becomes obvious that Russia has significant interests in exploiting disagreements among stakeholders to disrupt alternative routes.

With regards to security, like most Western states, Russia and China must also combat terrorism. During the Syrian Civil War, thousands of militants from both countries flocked into Syria to join numerous Islamist groups. Although the ISIS utilization of foreign fighters was brought to a halt, domestic radicalization remains an issue.

Domestic radicalization and self-determination movements assure that both Moscow and Beijing will be committed in counterterrorism activities. However, disagreements arise over the definition of "terrorism" and significantly decrease cooperation. Indeed, besides acknowledging common foes like ISIS, the U.S. labels many groups, such as Hezbollah or Hamas, as "terrorists." For their part, it is not likely that China and Russia will classify them as such. Therefore, in the case of regional conflicts, many of these groups could easily become instruments of future proxy competition, which complicates the scenario further.

Despite propaganda assertions that are primarily aimed at domestic audiences, attributing a proxy's military action to one of its funding providers is hardly a safe bet.

Robert Malley, Chief Executive Officer of the International Crisis Group and former White House Middle East Coordinator and Senior Advisor on Countering the Islamic State during the Obama administration, correctly states that we might be over-estimating the effective control that finance providers have over their proxies. The typical "state control" system that we have in the Western world hardly applies to the Middle East, where you have "states" that don't have any authority over large parts of their territory, as well as non-state actors, such as ISIS, the Kurds, Hezbollah, and the Houthis, which function like states. Funding providers might obtain access and safety in return, but they might not have a lot of influence over the proxies' military decision-making.

The U.S. withdrawal from Syria has increased the expectations from Russia. Therefore, the current situation has turned into an opportunity to expose Beijing's indifference to global issues and Moscow's weakness as a security provider.

China does not actually see Asia and the Middle East as different areas requiring different policies, in contrast to the U.S. vision. China considers the economic control of the Eurasian heartland as important for further expansion. In addition, China believes that Washington is pursuing an *"encirclement strategy"* that China must counteract.

From the Chinese perspective, the U.S.-led *"democratization"* is not just a struggle for values but also a means to reduce China's strategic reach on the Eurasian continent. Therefore, Beijing sees Central Asian countries and the Middle East, especially Iran, as the areas where U.S. influence and isolation attempts should be thwarted. According to China, Iran is the last country of the Greater Middle East that is preventing U.S. dominance in the strategically vital region linking the Middle East, Turkey, Afghanistan, and reaching into Central Asia.

Despite the average Middle Easterner's admiration of the American founding values—personal and political freedom—Arabs' popular opinion toward the U.S. is gradually shifting.

I am not a believer In the absolute accuracy of public opinion polls in the Middle East, however, a 2006 Arab public opinion poll, conducted by *Zogby International* and the Brookings Institution, showed that China, second only to France, is the country that most Arabs would like to see emerge as a superpower. The U.S. placed only fifth in the same poll. Hence, many wished to see the U.S. presence and influence in the region greatly reduced and see China as a potential check toward what many Arabs see as an overbearing and unreliable American foreign policy. Things might have changed since 2006, especially with regard to the Arabs' preference for France.

Also, because of the already-mentioned issue of Israel's perceived occupation of Palestinian lands, Arabs and Muslims harbor a deep resentment against the U.S. for its unwavering support to Tel Aviv. China's vocal support for the Palestinian cause and willingness to challenge the U.S. on a host of regional issues provide Arabs with a sense of hope. Beijing and Moscow immediately expressed support for the Arab Peace Initiative, the two-state solution: the establishment of a fully independent Palestinian state based on the 1967 borders, with East Jerusalem as its capital, thus paving the way for further involvement.

Afterword

"La Storia siamo noi...Nessuno si senta escluso...
Però la Storia non si ferma davvero...La Storia
dà torto o dà ragione. Siamo noi che abbiamo
tutto da vincere e tutto da perdere...Perché
è la gente che fa la Storia... Quelli che hanno
letto un milione di libri, e quelli che non
sanno nemmeno parlare. Ed è per questo che
la Storia dà i brividi, perché nessuno la può
negare La Storia siamo noi, siamo noi padri e
figli. La Storia non ha nascondigli. La Storia
non passa la mano. La Storia siamo noi"

We all are history's protagonists. No one should
feel excluded. Even if history does nor really
pause for us, if it assigns right and wrong, even
if it is us, the protagonists, who have everything
to gain or to lose, it is we who make history.
Those of us who have read millions of books,
and those who can't even speak properly.
That is why history gives you chills. Because
none of us can deny it, parents or progeny,
our role in history can't be hidden. In history
you can't pass a hand. History is us.

Francesco de Gregori—*La Storia Siamo Noi*

IN 2017, I WAS ATTENDING a meeting with U.S. Army Lieutenant
General (Ret.) *Terry Wolff,* U.S. Army Colonel *William "Bill"*

Mandrick, who was my direct boss at the time, and several foreign military officers, in Tampa, Florida.

Bill Mandrick is a no-nonsense infantry and Civil Affairs officer. An extremely sharp mind with a Doctorate in Philosophy, Bill could apply his cerebral reasoning to any complicated issue, and, after dissecting its intricacies, he would make it easier to tackle.

Terry Wolff had completed 34 years of military service, ending as the Director of Strategic Plans and Policy, for the U.S. Chairman of the Joint Chiefs of Staff. He had accumulated extensive experience in Washington, DC, working on military strategy, policy matters, and inter-agency affairs. He had served on the National Security Council as a Special Assistant to the President and Senior Director for Iraq and Afghanistan, and as a Deputy Special Presidential Envoy, working as part of the Obama and Trump administrations.

He met us, in his capacity as Deputy Special Presidential Envoy for the Global Coalition to Defeat ISIS. He was the policy and strategy buff; we were his front- and second-line operators in the fight against The Caliphate. We were going to finally find out how our civilian leadership saw the conflict, directly from the top.

His briefing started very well; Wolff is a very effective presenter. With the help of a very detailed PowerPoint slide deck, he started by describing the historical progress from the beginning of the campaign against The Caliphate to that present time. Suddenly, the shoe dropped.

When he went into the description of "Phase Four," the end-state, stabilization, and normalization of a post-ISIS Iraq (and Syria), he lost his entire audience. Very little made sense; it felt like he had forgotten his entire knowledge of the Middle East.

I vividly remember the perplexed looks on the foreign officers' faces, and the kicks that Bill Mandrick and I kept exchanging under the table, almost as we were trying to wake each other up from a bad dream. The truth was that we were extremely disappointed; we felt misrepresented. How could a few military officers, far below Wolff's pay grade, have a better understanding of the situation? Was the capital's rarefied policy atmosphere really that distant from the reality on the ground? How could the gap between political intentions and ground reality be so wide?

Wolff was talking about the nonexistent billions of dollars that the coalition was willing to provide for reconstruction in Iraq. He was assuming that, once the physical Caliphate had been destroyed, the reasons for its origin would have been successfully addressed, too. In that moment, one of America's foreign policy's best brains had failed to show an understanding of the international coalition's intentions and capabilities. He had failed to connect the dots of the global ramifications that the advent of The Caliphate had unleashed. End-state objectives should not be planned without the input of all the involved nations. Plans that determine the crafting of medium- to long-term foreign policies should not be built on thin air.

Whether his presentation was more of a political pitch than a strategic plan, we shall never know.

I hope that this book was able to communicate how complex the game is in the Middle East. Once you break something, you own it. The Queen owns it. Britain and France were very crafty in shifting a liability that America voluntarily accepted for economic reasons.

We should keep playing by challenging our understanding of "end-state," because, by Middle Eastern timing standards, we are so early in the game that correctly defining what an appropriate end-state looks like is impossible.

Whether we like it or not, whether it suits political messaging or not, we are in it for the long run. Sustained engagement to build trust is the only way forward. The Queen has an appointment with the history of the Middle East, and it must keep that appointment. Consistent, genuine human connection is at the base of everything in life. Keeping that appointment validates the Queen's commitment to this rule.

In an 8 February 2019 journal entry, I attempted to define that human connection: "...*whether it is a group of people from different parts of the world* (international coalition members) *dining in a Kuwaiti bazaar, who welcome one of the locals in their group photo, and connect across borders which are incongruent with the oneness of our nature—a day which makes you remember when every single human connection meant something deeper, opening our hearts and expanding our souls. Who should I send? Send me. And once I am on the way, help me keep an accepting, emphatic peripheral vision rather than be tunnel focused on a destination—an end state which I might not fully understand.*

There is no going back. If we do not have the courage and determination to change the way we look at the Middle East, I will leave it to the words of U.S. Army Sergeant Major *Basil Plumley* to sound the warning.

Immortalized in the 2002 movie *We Were Soldiers*, about the 1965 battle of *Ia Drang*—the first clash between a force of U.S. troops and the People's Army of Vietnam (NVA), which was the start of America's commitment to the Vietnam War—Plumley, while about to face an onslaught of attacking NVA soldiers, instructed the young troopers in his charge:

"Gentlemen, prepare to defend yourselves!"